Business Leaders:
The Faces Behind Beauty

Bu$ine$$ Leader$
The Faces Behind Beauty

Wanda Langley

MORGAN
REYNOLDS

PUBLISHING

Greensboro, North Carolina

Bu$ine$$ Leader$:

Russell Simmons
Steve Jobs
Oprah Winfrey
Warren Buffett
Michael Dell
Ralph Lauren
Faces Behind Beauty

BUSINESS LEADERS: THE FACES BEHIND BEAUTY

Copyright © 2009 By Wanda Langley

Library of Congress Cataloging-in-Publication Data

Langley, Wanda.
  Business leaders : the faces behind beauty / by Wanda Langley.
    p. cm.
  Includes bibliographical references and index.
  ISBN-13: 978-1-59935-097-4
  ISBN-10: 1-59935-097-1
  1. Cosmetics industry--United States--History. 2. Businesswomen--United States--Biography. 3. Beauty culture--United States--History.
I. Title.
  HD9970.5.C672L36 2008
  338.4'7668550922--dc22
                              2008018681

Printed in the United States of America
First Edition

*To Betty, Lynn, and Gene—the most
beautiful women I know*

Contents

Poro Hair and Beauty Culture *(Courtesy of New York Pubic Library)*

ONE

Beauty and Business

The search for beauty has been a changing, but endless quest. Throughout the ages, people have attempted to beautify themselves with the clothing they wore, the paint they applied to their bodies, and the way they have styled their hair. These standards of beauty have differed from age to age and from culture to culture, but the desire for beauty has persisted in all societies.

Indigenous people adorned themselves with paints made from plant and mineral dyes. Tribes in Africa used body paints and had elaborate hairstyles. Some cut the skin until the scars made detailed patterns on their bodies; others pierced their skin and tattooed themselves. Peoples in Asia and the Pacific islands also had intricate tattoos, which indicated rank and status in that society. In India and the Middle East, women applied henna patterns to their skins, a beautification method that is still used.

Not all body paint was for self-gratification. Sometimes it was part of religious practices or to mark important life's passages, such as birth, adulthood, marriage, and death. Native peoples of South America, Central America, and North America wore paint to ward off evil. Medicine doctors applied color to their bodies before ceremonies, and young men painted their faces before battle. Some Native American tribes used tattoos, and they smeared colored mud or sand over their bodies. This covering served to protect the skin against the sun and against biting insects.

Ancient civilizations around the Mediterranean Sea used paints to adorn themselves. Egyptians used kohl, a dark, lead-based mixture, to outline their eyes; they also smeared their eyelids with ground malachite, a vivid green metal, which also protected the eyelids from the sun. During the reigns of the Rameses and the Ptolemes, Egyptians used red carmine on their mouths and yellow ochre on their faces. Women spread on egg whites to prevent wrinkles.

Later Mediterranean societies also beautified themselves. Greek women of high status did not use cosmetics on their faces, but they had elaborate hairdos, curled by tongs. They dyed their hair blond by mixing potassium and flower petals; during periods of mourning they colored their hair black. Greek men used scented oils after they bathed. Cretes and Etruscans used whitener on their skins, applied makeup to their faces, and wore fancy hairstyles. Romans used makeup, which they brought from Egypt. Both men and women dyed their hair. Men also curled their hair and used perfumes.

The French were the first Europeans to wear makeup. King Henry III of France, who reigned from 1574 to 1589, plucked his eyebrows and painted his face red and white. Members of the royal court, male and female, wore makeup. Women used kohl eyeliner and put belladonna, a member of the deadly nightshade family, on their eyelids to illuminate their eyes. They curled their hair with hot irons, stuck in false hair, and held the coiffure together with pomade, an oily perfumed ointment. Even French nuns dyed and curled their hair.

Elizabeth I, Queen of England from 1558-1603, wore makeup and dyed her hair; her court members followed suit. Women used gold dust or the spice turmeric to color their hair blond and reddened their lips with cinnabar, which contained toxic mercury. To achieve an even, white complexion, wealthy women painted their faces and other exposed parts of their upper bodies with costly ceruse, a mixture of white lead and water or wine. This makeup had ghastly consequences. If used for a prolonged period, ceruse caused the hair and teeth to fall out, damaged internal organs, and rotted the face from the inside out. Eventually, a long-term user died of lead poisoning. Poorer women used a solution of borax and sulfur to lighten skin blemishes and colored their lips with a harmless (if unappealing) mixture of gum Arabic, boiled egg white, and ground cochineal, a red insect.

By the eighteenth century, European middle-class women began wearing color on the face. Eventually, tradesmen began to make and sell skin washes, which came with brand names. However, most women made their facial creams from recipes printed in domestic manuals. *The English Physician* contained a recipe that called for goat hair mixed with dung, minced veal, milk, cucumber water, and lemon juice.

When Europeans began to colonize North America they brought their beauty recipes with them. These recipes remained the domain of women and many learned how to use

Elizabeth I, Queen of England from 1558 to 1603, wore cosmetics and used hair dye. *(Courtesy of IMAGNO/Austrian Archives/Getty Images)*

herbs and other plants to treat skin disorders and to make skin lovelier. They passed their skin care recipes on to daughters and shared them with friends and neighbors.

In the nineteenth century, beauty recipes began to appear in domestic manuals and even cookbooks; most contained ingredients for creams, lotions, and astringents. Women who made their own products became known as "kitchen psychics" and protective lotions and creams were called "cosmetics." Rouge and other colors used on the face were known as "paints." Not until the twentieth century did facial makeup become called cosmetics (derived from a Greek word, meaning "skilled in adornment").

One of the earliest commercial makers of beauty aids in the United States was T. W. Dyott of Philadelphia, Pennsylvania. In 1814, he made powders, lotions, and hair pomades that he distributed along the Eastern seaboard. Other not-so-reputable local companies started making skin products and hired agents to sell their questionable goods to drugstores, grocery stores, and house to house. The companies placed ads in newspapers, women's magazines, and farm journals and also developed mail-order businesses to reach rural women. Their products became known as "patent cosmetics," and most of the contents were not all beneficial and some contained toxic mercury or lead.

Regular hair care was problematic during the nineteenth century. Women washed their hair about once a month. To clean their hair, they dissolved bits of soap into water, but the soap dried and frizzed the hair. Wealthy women had their servants do their hair, while poorer females washed their own. A woman kept her hairstyle simple and pulled it back or up into a bun; at night, she braided her hair before going to bed.

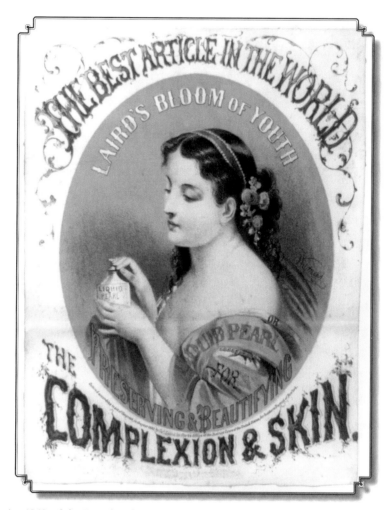

An 1863 ad for Laird's Bloom of Youth skin conditioner *(Library of Congress)*

By the mid-nineteenth century, a few women made a living by going to women's homes and dressing their hair. Some skilled black hairdressers went into homes of white women to do their hair.

Some African Americans wanted their curly hair straightened and some white-owned companies made hair-straightening products, such as Kink-No-More. These companies also sold skin lighteners, which often contained mercury or lead.

The use of these products caused controversy in the black communities. Editorials in black newspapers denounced these hair-straightening and skin-bleaching companies, although they often carried their ads in their newspapers because they needed the revenue. African American leaders said black women should not try to look like white women; from their pulpits, black ministers railed against these products. Even African American women differed. Activist Nannie Burroughs said, "What every woman who bleaches and straightens out needs, is not her appearance changed, but her mind changed." Soon, however, black-owned beauty companies sprang up to meet the growing demand for hair and beauty products.

A nineteenth-century cosmetic advertisement for hair oil *(Library of Congress)*

More commercial companies selling beauty aids entered the business in the later half of the nineteenth century. In 1882, Andrew Jergens, a soap-maker, started producing creams and lotions. Four years later, David Hall McConnell

A young woman powdering her face in 1877 *(Courtesy of The Bridgeman Art Library/Getty Images)*

started the California Perfume Company, later named Avon. In 1886, Harriet Hubbard Ayers began manufacturing her emollients. And in 1892, chemist Theron Pond produced toiletries and cold cream, so-called because air touching the cream created a cooling effect on the skin. These skin-care companies increased their marketing and promotion by advertising widely in newspapers and women's magazines. (Soap companies are credited with originating mass advertising in the United States.)

With the advent of photography, everyone wanted their image preserved, and they went to photography studios to have their pictures made. Studios had paints of rouge and lip color to enhance the woman's appearance in her photo. In 1894, the Sears & Roebuck Company catalogue sold its own brand of makeup, which included rouge and eyebrow pencil.

There was no stopping the growing demand for beauty products. During the twentieth century, when more women began entering the work force and business world, it created a bigger demand. More companies sprang up to fill this market. Annie M. Malone and Madam C. J. Walker made beauty products to serve the needs of African American women, Canadian-born Martha Matilda Harper developed an international franchise system of hair care, and Helena Rubinstein and Elizabeth Arden, two founders of the modern-day beauty industry, helped to make wearing cosmetics acceptable. They were followed by Estée Lauder who dominated the market during the last third of the twentieth century.

With clear ambition and rare business acumen, these women were able to build world-renowned business empires out of the poorest and most meager circumstances. As bosses, they were often highly demanding of their employees, but this was an essential component of their success. In some cases, it was necessary for these business leaders to be stricter and more rigorous than their male counterparts: these women faced not only the astounding challenge of building a successful business, but they had to do so at a time when women were not even legally allowed to vote and were expected to simply stay home. But through untiring effort and work, all six of these women were able to create businesses that not only made them stunningly wealthy and influential, but changed the course of business in America for all people.

TWO

Martha Matilda Harper

When Martha Matilda Harper was seven, her father sent her away. He had accumulated a large amount of debt and needed the money she could earn as a servant girl. The child went to work in the home of her maternal uncle and three aunts who lived about sixty miles away.

As a domestic servant, she was expected to labor thirteen to fifteen hours a day, cooking, washing, and cleaning for four adults. But as painful as that early experience was, she did learn the value of providing good service that would be necessary later when she became a hair-and-skin-care entrepreneur.

Martha Harper was born September 10, 1857, in Munn's Corner, a village north of Oakville, Ontario, in Canada. Her mother Beady bore ten children; Martha was the fourth. The family lived in a one-room cabin on a small plot of ground. Her father Robert Harper, a tailor by trade, did not work.

He paid little attention to his children, Martha in particular, and when he ran up large debts from speculating in land, he farmed all his children out as servants.

Teenaged girls from poor families were often "bound out" as servants. It was less common for a child to be sent away to do domestic labor at such a young age. The new "master" acted as parent, providing food, clothing, lodging, and a small salary was sent home to her family. Domestics had sparsely furnished rooms, usually in the attic or basement. They had a half day off each week and earned between three and four dollars a month. They were expected to show obedience and respect to their employers at all times. Female house servants had a grueling schedule: in the morning, arise no later than six a.m., light fires, prepare household breakfast, carry in water and wood, wash dishes, clean bedrooms, and run errands; in the afternoon, prepare midday meal, clean kitchen, dust, sweep, and do any other chores; in the evening, prepare and serve dinner, clean and straighten kitchen, then to bed to rest for the next day. In spite of the workload, the biggest problem any servant girl faced was the isolation and loneliness.

At about the age of twelve, Martha went to work as a housekeeper for a doctor in Orono, a neighboring village. Her new boss was interested in scalp and hair care. He taught Martha about the physiology of the scalp, stressing cleanliness as the basis for a healthy scalp and hair. He had also developed a special hair tonic that contained herbs and showed Martha how to shampoo her scalp with an olive oil-based soap and how to apply the special tonic on the hair and rinse with warm water. Before she left his house the doctor gave Martha the recipe for his secret-formula tonic.

In 1882, twenty-five-year-old Martha Harper decided to move to Rochester, New York, a bustling town of about 90,000 people seventy-five miles across Lake Ontario. She knew no one there, but she had long looked to the United States as the land of opportunity. When Harper bought a one-way ticket on a steamship bound for Rochester, she took with her a brown ceramic jug full of the hair tonic. In a knotted handkerchief, she carried the formula recipe and sixty silver dollars, her life's savings.

In Rochester, Harper worked as a maid in the home of an attorney and continued to send money to her family. When the attorney sold the house to Owen and Luella Roberts, Harper stayed on as their maid. She ended up looking after Luella Roberts, who became a mother figure to Harper, for forty-two years.

One of Harper's duties included grooming Mrs. Roberts' hair. When Mrs. Roberts' friends saw her beautifully kept gray hair, they wanted Harper to treat their hair. Mrs. Roberts allowed Harper to begin to make the herbal tonic in a tool shed behind the house.

As she worked mixing the tonic, Harper began to develop a marketing strategy to sell her product. Soon she had a friend sell it door-to-door during the day. But working all day caring for Mrs. Roberts, and working all night mixing the tonic, soon took a toll on her health. She had worked herself to physical exhaustion.

Around this time Harper became interested in Christian Science, a religion founded in the late 1870s by Mary Baker Eddy. One important principle of Christian Science was—and still is—a faith in the power of divine healing. Mrs. Eddy, once sickly and frail, was convinced she had come to wellness through a study of the Bible and a belief in the power of the mind to heal the body. To ward off illnesses, she emphasized the practice of physical, mental, and spiritual health, though she shunned medicine and doctors. When Harper regained her health, she attributed it to her new Christian Science beliefs and began incorporating Christian Science teachings into her beauty-business philosophy. To her, beauty meant good health and spiritual wholesomeness. She believed a healthy woman was a beautiful woman. "Beauty and health are inseparable," she said.

After six years of giving shampoos and facials in the Roberts' home, Harper decided to open her own hair-care shop. She wanted to rent a space in the largest building on Main Street in downtown Rochester, but Daniel Powers, owner of the building, would not give her a lease because he thought her shop would attract prostitutes. Harper hired attorney John Van Voorhis, a civil-rights advocate, to argue her case. Powers finally agreed to give a month-to-month lease, but he reserved the right to close the shop if it attracted the wrong clientele.

Martha Harper carefully planned her new business venture. She secured a patent on her hair tonic, named Mascaro Tonique for the Hair. She also adopted a logo, a cornucopia, and had the trademark registered. A photographer in the building noticed Harper and asked if he could take a picture of her with her floor-length hair. To attract customers, she put the striking photo on her shop door. This picture would become her most famous marketing tool.

In August 1888, thirty-one-year-old Harper opened her business with her life's savings: $360. The Harper Hairdressing Parlor became the first beauty shop in Rochester and one of only a handful in the United States. For a female to become a business owner was an extraordinary achievement in the nineteenth century. Few women in America owned businesses of any kind, with the exception of dressmakers and milliners who made hats. While women ran their own households, they still remained financially dependent on their husbands, unless they had inherited wealth. Women could not borrow money from banks, or vote.

In the beginning, Harper's business was slow. Her first customer was an artist who had a studio in the same building. When Harper learned the music teacher next door had no space for his students or their mothers to wait, she offered to share her waiting room. The mothers had their hair done while they waited on their children's music lessons. They spread the word about her attentive care and quality service.

In her shop, Harper paid careful attention to details. Her reception room had a blue chenille carpet, which she insisted be cleaned in the corners and underneath the edges. The new shop owner also developed a number of innovations. She had a marble sink cut on one side to fit a woman's neck; she also designed a wicker shampoo chair that reclined at different angles (though she failed to file a patent on this). To wash customers' hair, she had to haul water from a tap in the hallway.

Harper also developed a unique beauty-treatment method. After shampooing with the tonic and a rinse, she used a fine-tooth comb to clean the hair. The treatment also included a scalp massage to stimulate blood flow. The patron's hair could be styled, or the client could do her own. Harper also gave a massage, beginning with the chest and continuing upwards to the chin, temples, and areas around the nose and eyes. She applied a facial mask, followed by warm and cold towels. She also included a hand massage. The two-hour treatment gave the customer a sense of calmness and well-being. "Not just a hairdo, but peace," Harper said.

Word-of-mouth from satisfied patrons brought in more customers. Susan B. Anthony came for treatments. The famous

Susan B. Anthony, a famous suffragist, patronized the Harper Hairdressing Parlor and praised Harper's business skills. *(Library of Congress)*

suffragist reportedly pointed to Martha Matilda Harper as an example of a woman controlling her own destiny. As her business grew, the shop owner rented more room and hired more help. By 1890, she had hired five assistants, whom she personally trained. With money made from her shop, she hired tutors to teach her history, English, and art. Later, she took evening classes at the University of Rochester. She learned to enjoy Shakespeare and the opera.

Harper's customers in Rochester began to bring their out-of-town friends, one of whom was Mabel Gardiner Hubbard, wife of Alexander Graham Bell, from Washington, D.C. These influential women asked Harper to open shops in their own hometowns. In 1891, Harper set up a branch shop in Buffalo, New York, and put her sister Harriet in charge. A year later, she opened hair salons in Chicago, Illinois, and Detroit, Michigan. Bertha Farquhar, a Harper assistant headed the Chicago salon. Farquhar, a former servant herself, had a superb business sense and made her shop highly successful. Later, Harper asked her niece Nell Harper to manage the Rochester salon.

Harper trained the shop operators in her method of beauty care. She used her money to set up these trainees in businesses and taught them how to run them. In return, the operators gave a portion of their profits to Harper until she was paid back. When the debt was repaid, they owned the shops free and clear. However, they had to use the Harper Method products and equipment if they used her name. She also offered ongoing training and group insurance.

This system of satellite businesses, individually owned but operating under one name, is known today as franchising, which is derived from a French word meaning "freedom

Mabel Gardiner Hubbard, wife of Alexander Graham Bell, came from out of town to receive treatments at Harper's Rochester salon. *(Library of Congress)*

from servitude." Martha Matilda Harper became the first woman—and is believed to be the first person—to create a retail franchise in the United States. Ray Kroc, founder of McDonalds in 1951, developed the best-known franchise in the United States.

Harper was careful about whom she chose to head the franchises. She wanted them to be willing to work hard and know how to please the customer. Harper, a former house-maid, particularly sought out women who wanted to improve

Harper created the first franchise business in the U.S., a system that McDonald's founder Ray Kroc would later use to great success. *(Courtesy of Evelyn Hofer/Time Life Pictures/Getty Images)*

their station in life by becoming business owners. Each operator had to be pleasant-looking, have a good personality, and possess a temperament suited to the demands of running a business. The new business owners came to be known as "Harperites," and Harper fostered a sense of community among her "girls."

Absolute cleanliness was another must in the Harper Method shops. Operators wore white uniforms, aprons, and white hats, similar to how nurses dressed. Most important of all was customer service. In an interview with the *Christian Science Monitor,* Harper said, "Build everything on service. If you give full measure of service, you'll never want and your horn of plenty will overflow."

Soon, Harper was able to expand her business beyond the United States. In 1905, she opened her first Canadian shop in Toronto. Four years later, she had a salon in Berlin, Germany. By 1914, she had 134 franchises in 128 cities in the United States, Canada, and Europe. Harper traveled to her franchises to help with problems, and to make certain the shops used her products and maintained a high quality of customer service. She told her Harperites, "take people the way they are, not just the way you wish they were, for we are all just as we are . . . even the skunks."

In the summer of 1912, Harper took her first extended vacation. She and two of her shop owners made a trip to Yellowstone National Park. There, she met a guide and stagecoach driver named Robert Arthur MacBain. A Washington state high-school science teacher, he had taken the Yellowstone job during the summer season. MacBain, a native Iowan, had a slender face with blue eyes. He also had a flair for storytelling. Harper kept in touch with MacBain when she returned home. Then in 1916, he moved to Rochester and worked as Harper's executive assistant. Two years later, he enlisted in the United States Army during World War I, but later rejoined Harper in her business enterprise. The two married October 27, 1920. Captain Robert MacBain was thirty-nine; Martha Matilda Harper was sixty-three. She gave her age as ten years younger.

Family and friends of the couple expressed misgivings about the marriage. They assumed MacBain married Harper for her money. But the marriage benefited both. By becoming his wife's trusted administrator, MacBain could use his organizational talents. The marriage also allowed Harper to become a U.S. citizen. Furthermore, the couple treated each other with respect and affection. "Robbie always looks out for me," she said.

An 1905 view of Rochester, NY *(Library of Congress)*

In 1921, Harper established a formal hair-care training school in Rochester and appointed her niece, Ann Harper, to run the six-month program. She later opened other training schools across the United States and Canada. Every two months, a new class of ten to fifteen students entered the program. She had international students from Uruguay and even one woman from Baghdad, Iraq. Trainees first studied anatomy and hygiene. Then they learned how to do shampoo and scalp treatments, rinses and comb-outs, hair styling, and massages. Finally, they studied good business management. When the graduates became franchise owners, Harper gave each a lamp base shaped like a brown jug, similar to the tonic container she had first brought to America.

Harper decided she needed larger manufacturing facilities and headquarters for her booming business. Putting her husband in charge of the building program, she began construction of her headquarters in 1921. Harper placed her greatest treasures in the building cornerstone: the first fifty-cent piece she had earned, copies of Harper patent and product labels, and pictures of her early Harper associates. The last two items included the Bible and a copy of Mary Baker Eddy's *Science and Health*. Harper said, "We have laid a foundation today, not of stone, mortar, brick, or any other material substance. We have laid a spiritual foundation upon which, during my whole lifetime, I have tried to build the Harper Method . . . [It] was founded on Principle and Truth, and . . . it had succeeded . . . only because it had such a foundation."

MacBain called the new headquarters, which opened in 1922, The Laboratory. The company expanded its line of natural hair-care and skin-care products, and Harper Method, Inc.

Mary Baker Eddy *(Library of Congress)*

flourished. In 1923, more than three hundred Harper shops operated worldwide; by 1927, there were five hundred.

During the first two decades of the twentieth century rapid changes came to the beauty business. Black women entrepreneurs, such as Annie Turnbo Malone and Madam C. J. Walker, produced their own products. Helena Rubinstein and

Elizabeth Arden, who emphasized facial cosmetics, began giant beauty businesses in New York. Women had begun to wear makeup, rouge, and lipstick, and wanted their hair cut short, dyed, and curled. Martha at first resisted the hair bobs because she thought repeated cuttings would cause baldness. She finally offered the short haircuts, but would not do permanents, believing the harsh chemicals would damage the hair. She used only organic dyes, such as henna, which she applied to her own hair.

Some Harper shop owners began to stray from her methods and introduce new cosmetics and other types of hair care. In her newsletter, the *Harper Method Progress*, she said, "The Harper Method represents a standard of work that is worth patterning after . . . I want Harperites everywhere to realize that sticking to the Harper Method faithfully, day in and day out, is the wisest thing they can do." If the shop owners did not follow her standards, she withdrew her support and made them stop using her name.

Harper also developed a product for baldness, which attracted men to her shops. However, the male patrons, many of whom were business executives, had separate rooms for their scalp treatments. They also had massages and facials. When President Woodrow Wilson traveled to Europe after World War I, he stopped for a massage and hair treatment in the Paris salon. President Calvin Coolidge was so pleased with his treatment that he had Harper Method equipment and products put into the White House. Several First Ladies, including Jacqueline Kennedy, also enjoyed Harper treatments.

Harper came up with another shrewd innovation—she provided play areas for the children as their mothers had their hair done. Harper also cultivated children as potential customers.

President Calvin Coolidge had Harper Method equipment and products in the White House. *(Library of Congress)*

She told her shop owners: "The child in your Shop should be treated as an intelligent individual . . . Have a corner in your Shop for this important clientele, fitted with a little chair and table and a plaything or two . . . Small patrons of the present make the most loyal and persistent patrons of the future."

By all accounts, Martha Matilda Harper was kind and generous. She once gave seventy-five cents to one of her nieces, and when the girl bought a variety-store necklace with the money, her parents insisted she return it to the store. Harper took off her own necklace and put it around her niece's neck. In addition to caring for her former employer Luella Roberts, she also looked after her own family, giving her sisters and nieces important positions in her company. Harper showed another aspect of her character when twenty years after she became successful, she erected a large tombstone in Oakville cemetery to honor her mother and two deceased siblings; her father lay in an unmarked grave.

During the Great Depression of the 1930s, many beauty shops closed because clients had little money. Those salons that remained opened lowered their prices to keep their customers. But since Harper targeted an elite clientele, she kept her prices at seventy-five cents for a shampoo and set (the equivalent of about $8.30 today; in 1931, the average hourly wage for a woman was $.40 an hour). Her newspaper ads read, "HARPER SERVICE COST MORE—IS WORTH MORE." Harper claimed that none of her shops closed. However, she did adjust to changing economic conditions. She offered specials at certain times and on certain days when business was slow, opened her shops during evening hours so her business and professional patrons could get their hair done after work, and began to place her products in department stores.

In 1932, at the age of seventy-eight, Martha Harper promoted her husband to president of the company. She assumed the role of founder and vice-president. With the company now in his control, MacBain made changes. Harper shops finally offered hair permanents. New recruits were no longer servant girls. But the Harper Method shops continued to grow and to attract many well-known patrons, such as the great stage actress Helen Hayes, and Irene Dunn, a movie star, and comedians Danny Kaye and the Marx Brothers. The DuPont, Vanderbilt, and Hearst families also had Harper treatments. If requested, the Harperites went into the homes of some of their famous clients to give treatments.

In 1938, the company celebrated fifty years in business by throwing a Golden Jubilee. More than four hundred Harperites descended on Rochester. The mayor and other local dignitaries welcomed the crowd, and the MacBains later hosted a garden party. The devoted Harperites presented gifts to their eighty-one-year-old founder: a "throne" (gold brocade arm chair); a silver tea and coffee set; a gold mesh bag and fifty golden rosebuds. They also gave MacBain a leather bound set of works by Scottish writer Robert Burns.

Harper became increasingly detached from her company. She worked in her garden and began a long slide into senility. As her dementia worsened in the 1940s, MacBain turned company management over to others while he took care of his wife and her invalid sister. However, he kept Harper's condition a secret from the franchise owners. In 1948 at the company's sixtieth anniversary, she made her last appearance. Led in by MacBain, she smiled and waved to her cheering Harperites, then left, guided out by her husband.

Martha Matilda Harper died August 3, 1950, one month shy of her ninety-third birthday. She was buried in Riverside Cemetery at Rochester, New York. In her will, she left all her property and personal assets to her husband. In 1955, MacBain sold the company. He died a year later. After the sale, the company had all-male ownership. Harper Method, Inc. operated until 1972 when a Canadian firm bought the company; it retained the formulas for the original Harper products.

Harper never envisioned her empire as just a collection of businesses doing hair and selling products. "The Great Achievement of the Harper Empire is the women it has made," she once said.

In 2003, Harper was inducted into the National Women's Hall of Fame. Her former headquarters in Rochester has MARTHA MATILDA HARPER still etched on the front of the building. The Rochester Museum and Science Center now holds her archival collection, and in its Business Hall of Fame hangs a striking photo of young Martha Matilda Harper— with her magnificent hair cascading to the floor.

Martha Matilda Harper timeline

1857	Born in Oakville, (Ontario) Canada, on September 10.
1869- 1881	Employed by physician who teaches her hair-care methods.
1882	Migrates to Rochester, New York.
1888	Opens first hair salon in Rochester, New York, in August.
1891	Establishes a branch shop in Buffalo, New York.
1892	Opens hair-care franchises in Detroit, Michigan, and Chicago, Illinois.
1909	Opens the first Harper Method shop abroad in Berlin, Germany.
1920	Marries Robert Arthur MacBain and becomes a U.S. citizen.
1921	Establishes Harper Method training center in Rochester, New York.
1922	Opens new headquarters in Rochester, New York.

Illinois, with her children. After the war, Robert Turnbo joined them and started farming, but no records can be found of him ever holding deed or title to any land. Most accounts say her parents died before she started school. However, in the book *History of Massac County, Illinois,* Annie's older brother John L. Turnbo claimed his mother died in 1887 and his father in 1893.

At some point, Annie went to live with her older sister Laura Roberts. An unspecified illness forced her to drop out of school before she graduated. In the 1890s, Annie's family moved to southern Illinois to the all-black community of Lovejoy, now named Brooklyn. "When I was a little girl," she said, "I used to trot through the field around Lovejoy gathering herbs with an old woman relative of mine [who] was an herb doctor, and her mixtures fascinated me." She experimented with ingredients for a shampoo, and she worked on the hair of other African American women in the community.

Hairdressing among black women was as much a social occasion as it was a beauty ritual. They took great pleasure in hairstyling. The practice went back to Africa where women wore elaborately dressed hair in an infinite variety of styles. Often times the styles indicated a woman's status: a particular style might signify, for example, whether a woman was married, single, or engaged, or give clues about her age, religion, tribal affiliation, social status and wealth, or even the geographic area in which she lived.

During slavery, black women had neither the time nor the means to care for their hair, which resulted in serious problems, such as thinning hair and hair loss. They also suffered from scalp problems such as eczema, an inflammatory skin eruption, and psoriasis. A poor diet and lack of good hair care caused many of these conditions.

When hair-straightening techniques came into common practice, new challenges emerged. Many African American women wanted their naturally thick, and tightly twisted or curly hair to be smooth and full. To loosen the curl, they applied goose fat or axle grease to their hair, and then used a hot comb to straighten it. But this straightening method burned the hair, often causing it to break

Annie Turnbo Malone *(Courtesy of New York Public Library)*

off. Another straightening technique involved wrapping sections of the hair around strings and twisting them; this too could damage the hair, causing it to fall out.

Hair-straightening products sold on the market also led to scalp and hair damage. Turnbo was convinced she could develop a shampoo that would not harm hair. But first, she was convinced that healthy hair began with cleanliness.

In 1899, Turnbo rented a room in a small building in Lovejoy for $5.00 a month. There she mixed ingredients and came up with a shampoo she called the "Wonderful Hair Grower." She and her sister went door-to-door, selling her product to skeptical women. "I went out and made them change their mind," she said. "I went around in the buggy and made speeches, demonstrated the shampoo on myself, and talked about cleanliness and hygiene, until they realized I was right." About this time, she developed a disk-shaped, steel comb and a pressing iron for smoothing the hair. The United States Patent & Trademark Office has no records of her securing patents for these inventions.

In 1903, the city of St. Louis, Missouri, prepared to host the World's Fair in celebration of the one hundredth anniversary of the Louisiana Purchase. (It actually opened a year later.) Turnbo saw this upcoming event as a great business opportunity. In 1902, she rented a four-room apartment on Market Street in St. Louis where she offered hair treatments and developed her products. By this time, she had added a cleansing cream, moisturizer, and face powder.

Business took priority in Turnbo's life. In 1903, she married a man named Pope but divorced him a few years later because he tried "to interfere with her business."

The aspiring entrepreneur began recruiting other African American women as "agents," or saleswomen. The first thing she did was teach them how to use and demonstrate her products. Most of the women worked as domestics or washerwomen and welcomed the opportunity to do more dignified work at better pay. One of her first recruits was Sarah Breedlove McWilliams, who would later become known as Madam C. J. Walker. Turnbo claimed later that she helped McWilliams solve her own hair problems.

Turnbo decided to expand her market into the South. In 1904, she traveled to five southern states: Mississippi, Alabama, Georgia, Tennessee, and Arkansas. She spoke to black churches and black women's clubs where she gave free demonstrations and told women they could earn more selling her products than working as domestics or laboring in the fields. At her first church meeting in Mississippi, eleven people signed up to buy the products

A view of the 1903 World's Fair in St. Louis, Missouri *(Library of Congress)*

wholesale from Turnbo and sell them to their customers at retail prices.

According to a former employee, Turnbo paid about two and a half cents for the materials that went into a tin, which she then sold to her agents for twenty-five cents a tin. Agents, in turn, sold the product to their customers for fifty cents. Agents could make a minimum of two to three dollars a week; top-selling agents could earn more. Black domestic workers averaged about one dollar a week, and many made less. Turnbo reinvested her profits in the business and most of the agents did the same.

In 1906, Malone registered her trademark, "Poro," with the U.S. Patent Office, which would protect her company's name from being used by others. One source claims she coined the word from the combination of the first two letters in *Po*pe and *Ro*berts, her sister who helped her during her early years. Others say that Poro came from an African word in Liberia, meaning "spiritual and physical growth."

Turnbo's initial strategy of marketing her products is called direct selling, and the practice goes back to early civilizations. It offers advantages for both the sales force and the wholesaler. Those who sell can start their own ventures with little formal training and a minimum investment. Direct selling offers a flexible work schedule and better pay; it also gives recognition and reward to those who work hard. For the black companies, this business method did not require as great an initial investment or capital, which was almost impossible to obtain from white lending institutions at the time.

Turnbo soon faced unexpected competition from a former agent. Sarah McWilliams (Madam C. J. Walker) moved to Denver in 1905 and for a time, continued to sell Turnbo's products.

To counter Walker's competition, Turnbo also ran ads in the black newspapers, the *St. Louis Palladium* and the *Denver Statesman*:

> The proof of the value of our work is that we are being imitated and largely by persons whose own hair we have actually grown and the furthere [sic] fact that they have very frequently mentioned us when trying to sell their goods (saying that theirs 'is the same' or 'just as good') or referred to as 'PORO.' We advise you to use only 'PORO' Hair Grower (the oldest and best of its kind).

Turnbo traveled extensively, promoting her products and recruiting agents. By 1910, she had expanded into New York, Pennsylvania, Ohio, and Indiana. That same year, she moved into larger quarters on Pine Street in St. Louis. She opened a beauty shop where she trained other women in the Poro system of hair care. Students paid about $25.00-$35.00 for a course, which lasted several weeks. After training, they could operate their own beauty shops. Turnbo required her trainees to sign a contract, stating they would use only the Poro method and would sell only Poro products.

In 1910, Turnbo brought a lawsuit against one of her former students, Maggie Bedford, who had been one of her trainees in 1907. Bedford started her own hairdressing business, but she began using inferior products she had made herself. However, she continued to advertise that she had been trained in the Poro system. Turnbo filed a lawsuit, claiming that Bedford broke the terms of her contract, and that the inferior products she used had caused Poro's reputation to suffer. Turnbo won the suit. Bedford had to pay her $25 and agree not to advertise that she learned her hair-care system from Poro. This case became the first in a string of lawsuits filed by Turnbo, who was determined to protect both her company's reputation and its products.

She continued recruiting agents in other states. In turn, these agents recruited others to demonstrate and sell Poro. Her highly successful recruiting lay in her great ability to motivate people to sell her products. She established Poro schools and trained women in her method of hair care. Turnbo also operated a thriving mail-order business. To attract agents and buyers, she placed ads in black newspapers and magazines. However, she relied on word-of-mouth for most of her advertising. She had started her business without financial backing from family, friends, and banks, when pernicious racism and discrimination was a daunting obstacle to any black woman who attempted to establish a nationwide business. Her success was an extraordinary achievement.

Turnbo's success began to be recognized by other African American business leaders across the country. In 1913, she attended the fourteenth annual meeting of the National Negro Business League (NNBL) in Philadelphia, Pennsylvania. C. K. Robinson, publisher of the *Clarion* in St. Louis, introduced her as a "progressive businesswoman, who has built up . . . a large and magnificently appointed establishment devoted exclusively to hair culture."

In 1914, Turnbo married Aaron Eugene Malone, a former schoolteacher and Bible salesman. A handsome man, he possessed much energy, charm, and ambition. After their marriage, he declared he was leaving the Bible-selling business and joining his wife's firm. She made him manager and

Aaron Malone *(Courtesy of New York Public Library)*

president of Poro, while she devoted her time to recruiting and training. But soon the couple was struggling for control of the company, and the marriage would prove to be a personal and professional disaster.

Annie Malone decided to build a school of cosmetology, Poro College, in St. Louis. She bought a city block in an area known as "the Ville." The building was completed in 1917,

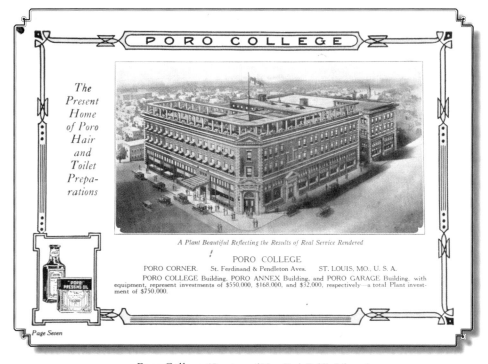

The
Present
Home
of Poro
Hair
and
Toilet
Prepa-
rations

A Plant Beautiful Reflecting the Results of Real Service Rendered

PORO COLLEGE.

PORO CORNER.   St. Ferdinand & Pendleton Aves.   ST. LOUIS, MO., U. S. A.
PORO COLLEGE Building, PORO ANNEX Building, and PORO GARAGE Building, with equipment, represent investments of $550,000, $168,000, and $32,000, respectively—a total Plant investment of $750,000.

Page Seven

Poro College *(Courtesy of New York Public Library)*

dedicated in 1918, and cost $500,000 to build. She paid for it in cash.

The building contained laboratories and a manufacturing plant, beauty shops, and a barbershop. It also housed a restaurant, an ice cream parlor, hotel rooms, a bakery, and a rooftop garden. Two years later, Malone added a $100,000 annex. When completed the complex was 100,000 square feet and became a meeting place—and a source of great pride—for black social, business, and professional groups.

Poro College also featured an eight hundred-seat auditorium and theater where many famous black entertainers performed, including singers Ethel Waters and Marian Anderson. Thomas Andrew Dorsey, a composer of gospel songs, wrote his hymn "Precious Lord Take My Hand" there, the location where he first heard about the death of his wife and child. Annie Malone herself loved hymns and organized a twenty-piece all-women Poro orchestra, which performed only religious music.

But the heart of Poro was the cosmetology school, which trained black beauticians. It stated as its purpose, "to lend beauty and charm to womanhood" and provided instruction on hair and skin care, including hair weaving, manicures, pedicures, and massages. Malone taught trainees how to dress and speak, and how to operate a business. After graduation, the graduates went out as Poro agents and "hair culturists" trained to operate beauty shops that used only Poro hair-care techniques and sold Poro products. Each shop constituted a Poro franchise. Annie Malone became the first African American woman to start a franchise system in the United States.

Poro employed nearly two hundred people, making it the largest black employer in St. Louis. Malone ran a tightly regimented work environment. She required all the women to wear white blouses and black skirts, and dressed conservatively herself. She did not tolerate much talking or dissent in the workplace. Some accused her of being autocratic, but Malone provided dignified and steady employment for African Americans. She also provided insurance benefits and low-cost mortgage financing to her employees, a rarity in the business world at that time.

Once a year she gave a Christmas party for her Poro agents and operators. She invited black newspapers editors to attend the glittering event. To agents who had worked for five years, she gave diamond rings. She also gave cash awards to top saleswomen and to those who bought houses

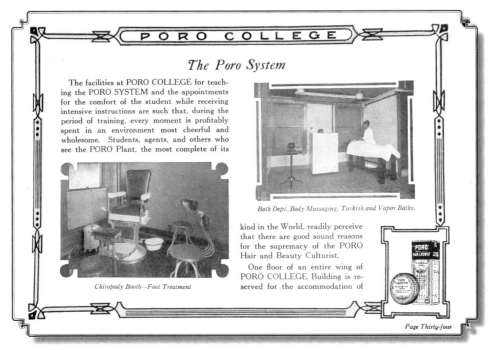

PORO COLLEGE

The Poro System

The facilities at PORO COLLEGE for teaching the PORO SYSTEM and the appointments for the comfort of the student while receiving intensive instructions are such that, during the period of training, every moment is profitably spent in an environment most cheerful and wholesome. Students, agents, and others who see the PORO Plant, the most complete of its

Bath Dept. Body Massaging. Turkish and Vapor Baths.

kind in the World, readily perceive that there are good sound reasons for the supremacy of the PORO Hair and Beauty Culturist.

One floor of an entire wing of PORO COLLEGE Building is reserved for the accommodation of

Chiropody Booth—Foot Treatment

Page Thirty-four

Photographs of different facilities at Poro College, where students were versed in the methods of the Poro System. *(Courtesy of New York Public Library)*

with their earnings. Agents who gave exceptional service to Poro received free trips.

Malone stressed the value of good service to her agents. "I urge you to give every customer the very best service you know how," she said, "Never disappoint a customer, make the surroundings attractive where you give the treatments, always keep enough PORO on hand to serve your customers." It was not enough for agents to just offer beauty services to women of color. She encouraged them to organize local clubs and to serve their communities. "It is our earnest wish that every PORO agent be an active force for good."

Annie Malone practiced what she preached. Almost from the beginning of her arrival in St. Louis, she had been involved in her community. She contributed large sums to St. James African Methodist Episcopal (AME) Church and to other black churches. She later served on the St. Louis Community Council and lobbied to have streets paved in the Ville. She gave much of her wealth over to social needs and causes. Malone particularly had a soft spot for orphans. According to sources, she gave $5,000 to every black orphanage in the United States and in 1922 donated a $10,000 plot of land to St. Louis Colored Orphans Home. She served as president of the orphanage from 1919-1943. It became known as the Annie Malone Children's Home in 1946.

Malone also gave generously to education, particularly to black colleges. She donated money to Tuskegee Institute and gave $30,000 to Howard College medical school, the largest sum of money ever given to any black institution in the country at that time. (In 1931, Howard University awarded her with an honorary Masters of Arts.) Malone also contributed to Mary McLeod Bethune's college in Daytona, Florida. It was reported, although not confirmed, that at one time she supported two students at every black land-grant college in the United States. She also paid for the education of her nieces and nephews. She said that her money "belonged to God, and should draw interest in human character."

By the mid-1920s, Malone's business brought in $5,000 a day. She had an estimated worth of $14,000,000, making her the second-wealthiest woman in St. Louis. (The richest was a white heiress.) Her chauffeur told a story of when she decided to buy a new car. She and the driver went into a Rolls Royce dealership. White salesmen ignored the black businesswoman, prompting her driver to finally ask for service. She placed an order for a Rolls Royce and wrote a check for the amount. Not believing an African American woman possessed that much money, the salesman phoned the bank to find out if her account held sufficient funds. Malone waited silently until he finished. Then she tore the check into little pieces and walked

Students on the campus of Howard University, circa 1946. Malone's donation of $30,000 to Howard medical school was the largest sum donated to any black institution in the country at the time. *(Courtesy of Alfred Eisenstaedt/Time Life Pictures/Getty Images)*

out. She directed her chauffeur to take her to a Pierce Arrow dealer, where she bought a new automobile on the spot—and paid cash.

In spite of her riches, Malone remained proudest of the economic opportunities she gave black women. She said:

> The entry of our colored women in business dates practically from the beginning of Poro. The army of 70,000 agents who represent Poro in every city and hamlet in the United States played an important part in the development of business and home life. The gospel of 'better personal appearance' has resulted in increased opportunities for service—families supported, the children educated, new ventures fianced [sic], living standards raised and wealth accumulated as a result of these efforts of these evangels of Poro.

From 1921 through 1926, Malone became involved in three separate court cases in which she alleged there had been trademark infringement by other companies. Although none of these companies used the Poro name, Malone thought these new trademarks sounded similar enough to create confusion and hurt Poro sales. She won two of these cases and lost the other. In each case, she had to hire lawyers who commanded huge fees. However, she would do whatever it took to protect her company.

Malone faced her biggest crisis in 1927 when her husband filed for divorce. He demanded one-half of her Poro holdings, claiming himself responsible for the company's success. She fought back. "That college . . . belongs to me to the last penny," she said. The divorce proceedings split the black community in St. Louis, and even African Americans nationwide. Aaron Malone had been active in the Missouri

Republican Party and in the black business community and had many high-placed friends who sided with him. Malone herself drew the support of local and national black women. Mary McLeod Bethune, president of the National Association of Colored Women (NACW), publicly backed her. Eventually, Malone settled the case by giving her husband $200,000 and a divorce; payments to her lawyers amounted to $100,000. She held on to Poro, but the company never recovered from the financial damage and negative publicity.

She had other problems. In 1929, Claude A. Barnett, influential founder and director of the United Negro Press, a Chicago-based news distribution company, wrote her a candid letter. He acknowledged her success: "That you are a splendid business woman, I am eager to agree." But he went on to say that "you are always surrounded with a group of sycophants. Everywhere you go people are eager to please you. They say only the things which they think you wish to hear and keep in their minds the disadvantages which might pique you."

Barnett was determined to tell her what was on his mind. He advised her to upgrade her products and keep the Poro name before the public by advertising. "Make the ads so tempting that every woman who does not use Poro will think she is missing something," he said, while also warning, "competition from white firms is constantly becoming keener."

Annie Malone decided to make a new start, and in 1928 bought an entire city block on Chicago's South Side on South Parkway, between Forty-fourth and Forty-fifth Streets. In 1930, she moved her headquarters to Chicago, though she kept her Poro building in St. Louis. However, the city of Chicago would not issue her a manufacturing license, and she had to contract some of her manufacturing out to other companies.

One of these firms, Proctor and Gamble Company, made Malone's brand of Poro soap. In 1933, the company decided to bring out its own soap called "Polo." When the patent examiner granted Proctor and Gamble a Polo trademark, Malone challenged the ruling. She thought this name was too similar to Poro, and she appealed the decision to the commissioner of patents. He sided with Proctor and Gamble. Malone directed her lawyers to file her case to the Court of Customs and Patent Appeals. The judges there reversed the commissioner's decision; Proctor and Gamble could not produce the Polo soap brand. She had a won a battle against a major American corporation.

In 1936, Malone suffered a setback when she lost a lawsuit brought against her by a former St. Louis employee. The case had its beginning in 1911 when she fired Walker L. Majors, her promoter. Four years later, he filed a lawsuit claiming a breach of contract. Malone would not pay, saying Majors refused to work under terms of his contract. The case wound through the legal system until 1936 when the Missouri Supreme Court ruled against Malone. The original lawsuit first brought in 1915 for the amount of $6,000 now totaled over $20,000 because of interest charges and court costs. Malone was already facing a serious cash flow problem and could not meet her mortgage payments on her original Poro building. In 1937, the St. Louis bank holding the mortgage foreclosed on the property. (Majors got nothing from his lawsuit.) One article read, "St. Louis Poro Building Passes to Whites." The loss struck a personal blow to Malone and the St. Louis black community.

Poro, headquartered in Chicago, continued to operate, but the problems mounted. Malone hired managers who did not serve the company's best interests, and trusted employees stole from her. From 1943-1951, the Internal Revenue Service (IRS) brought a series of lawsuits for failure to pay excise taxes the federal government levied against all cosmetics in 1924. She also failed to pay her real estate taxes in Chicago. Black business leaders stepped in to save Poro. Claude A. Barnett and C. C. Spaulding, president of the North Carolina Mutual Life Insurance and Company, made an offer to buy Poro Company. They would settle all company debts, bring in new managers, and keep Malone as a "figurehead" president. Her lawyer advised her to sell, but she refused to give up any control over her business and the deal fell apart. Barnett predicted it would be only a matter of time before Malone would lose her company.

Throughout the difficult times, Malone continued to be honored by those in her business. When the National Poro Dealers' Convention met annually, the agents, teachers, and dealers of the organization always paid homage to their founder. In 1950, they had a fiftieth anniversary celebration in Chicago. During this grand three-day affair, business and religious leaders paid her tributes. The National Convention of Beauty Culturist League acclaimed her "Pioneer Beauty Culturist."

In 1951, the IRS seized Poro and turned management over to outsiders, who promptly looted the company.

Annie Malone had lost her great empire due to several factors: a lack of control over finances, heavy costs due to involvement in lawsuits, failure to pay taxes, and the hiring of poor managers. C. C. Spaulding observed, "It is regrettable that Mrs. Malone did not have a competent business manager years ago." The *Chicago Defender* and *Pittsburgh Courier* also attributed part of the loss to her "overly generous" nature of giving money to many causes. Malone once said, "I have not been seeking money. I am only trying to help my race."

In 1955, under court supervision, two of Malone's nephews took over and reorganized Poro. The company operated until 1989, when the last beauty shop closed. During its almost ninety years of existence, Poro had established forty-eight beauty schools and one hundred beauty supply stations, covering the United States, Canada, Central America, the Caribbean, Africa, and the Philippines. The company also trained more than 100,000 cosmetologists, including Chuck Berry who took Poro hairdressing courses in St. Louis before he became a rock 'n' roll star.

After the loss of Poro, Annie M. Malone suffered from declining health and died of a stroke on May 10, 1957. She was eighty-seven years old. Her nieces and nephews, as well as devoted Poro agents, attended her funeral at Bethel African Methodist Episcopal Church in Chicago. She was buried in Burr Oak Cemetery.

At the time of her death Malone's personal fortune had dwindled to an estimated $100,000. A few months after her death, the *Pittsburgh Courier* ran a series of articles about Annie Turnbo Malone, calling her, "America's Original Beauty Queen." In its tribute to her, the newspaper said: "Annie Malone's life was a rich and beautiful life. She bequeathed to America's Negro women the beauty of well-manicured locks of hair. Her philanthropy helped many needy Negro youths to gain college educations. Her donations helped hundreds of social agencies to weather the storm of the depression."

In 1965, St. James AME Church razed the original Poro building to make way for senior citizens housing. But Malone was not forgotten. In the city where she started her business, people still tell the story of the beauty queen benefactor. A St. Louis street bears her name, as does the Annie Malone Children and Family Service Center. Every fourth Saturday in May, it has an Annie Malone March to raise funds. Today, the center offers a broad network of social services to the community. This spirit of giving remains one of Annie M. Turnbo Malone's greatest legacies.

Annie M. Turnbo Malone timeline

1869   Annie Minerva Turnbo born in Metropolis, Illinois, on August 9.

1902   Moves business to St. Louis, Missouri.

1904   Expands sales to the South.

1906   Registers Poro trademark.

1914   Marries Aaron E. Malone.

1918   Dedicates Poro College in St. Louis.

1922   Donates land to St. Louis orphanage.

1927   Divorces Aaron Malone.

1930   Moves headquarters to Chicago, Illinois.

1931   Awarded an honorary Masters of Arts by Howard College.

1933   Wins trademark lawsuit against Proctor and Gamble Co.

1936   Loses major lawsuit brought by former employee.

1937 Loses St. Louis Poro building to bank foreclosure.

1943-
1951 Involved in a series of lawsuits brought by Internal Revenue Service for failure to pay excise taxes.

1951 Poro company seized by federal government.

1957 Dies in Chicago, Illinois, on May 10.

FOUR

Madam C. J. Walker

When Madam C. J. Walker asked to address the 1912 National Negro Business League convention about what she had learned as a business operator, the organization's president Booker T. Washington ignored her request. Always determined, Walker stood up at the convention and said: "Surely, you are not going to shut the door in my face . . . I am a woman that came from the cotton fields of the South. I was promoted from there to the washtub. Then I was promoted to cook kitchen, and from there I promoted myself into the business of manufacturing hair goods and preparations . . . I have built my own factory on my own ground."

Madam C. J. Walker began life at the very bottom. She was born Sarah Breedlove on December 23, 1867, in Delta, Louisiana, almost two years after the Civil War. Her parents, Owen and Minerva Breedlove, and her four oldest siblings had been born into slavery. Only Sarah and her younger brother were freeborn.

Madam C. J. Walker *(Courtesy of Michael Ochs Archives/Getty Images)*

The family lived in a one-room shack on the Robert Burney cotton plantation where her parents worked as share-croppers. Sharecroppers had a plot of ground, which the owner let them work. He provided the tenants with seeds and supplies on credit and in return, the sharecroppers had to give him as much as two-thirds of their crop. They had to try to live on selling what was left. On years when the crops failed, which happened often, the sharecropper still owed for the seeds and supplies. In most cases the sharecroppers were deeply in debt to the owner and lived in what was essentially slavery for most of their lives.

In order to survive, the whole family worked in the fields. There was little time for education; Sarah estimated that she had three months of formal schooling total.

When Sarah was seven years old, her mother died. Two years later, her father passed away and she went to live with her sister and brother-in-law, where her life became more difficult. She described her brother-in-law as a "cruel man," but never elaborated further. They moved to Vicksburg, Mississippi, where the two sisters worked at washing clothes.

At the age of fourteen, Sarah married Moses McWilliams, a laborer. In 1885, she gave birth to their daughter Lelia. But her husband died about three years later. How he met his death is a mystery. According to some reports McWilliams was killed in a race riot; other reports claim that he was lynched—lynch mobs killed close to 2,500 black men, women, and children between 1882 and 1930 in ten southern states.

In early 1889, twenty-one-year old Sarah McWilliams and her daughter moved to St. Louis, Missouri, where she hoped to earn more money as a laundress than she could in Vicksburg. She was one of thousands of African Americans who left the Deep South in the years after the Civil War and migrated to larger cities in the mid- and upper South, as well as the North, in search of better wages. When she arrived in St. Louis, about 35,000 African Americans lived in the city, and some owned businesses. An estimated three hundred black men, including Sarah's brothers, gave their occupation as barbers. Most black women worked as domestics or washerwomen. At that time, ninety-nine percent of the washerwomen in St. Louis were African Americans.

A laundress toiled from sunup to sundown, six days a week. On Mondays, she picked up white customers' clothes and washed them in an iron pot over an open fire. She had to provide her own tubs, soap, and firewood. To clean the clothes, she used lye soap, a caustic substance that burned and chapped the hands. Then she beat the clothes with a stick or scrubbed them on a rub board. Finally, the laundry had to be rinsed in a wooden tub, starched, and hung on a line to dry. After ironing the articles, the washerwoman folded the clean laundry into a basket and delivered it back to the customers on Saturday. For this backbreaking work, she earned about $1.50 a day.

On Sundays, Sarah found inspiration and comfort at her church, St. Paul African Methodist Episcopal (AME), one of the largest African American houses of worship in St. Louis. St. Paul preached a lesson of self-help and advocated social and political causes. It also had an outreach program to the poor. For several days a week, Sarah sent Lelia to a school operated by women of the church.

In 1894, Sarah married John H. Davis. It was a difficult marriage almost from the beginning and her life grew even harder. Friends and neighbors described her husband as lazy and unwilling to hold a steady job. When he did work, he refused to share his wages with her. He also had affairs, drank heavily, and physically abused his wife. He was in and out of court for fighting and drunkenness. When the couple separated after nine years of marriage she never spoke of him again.

In spite of her meager earnings, Sarah managed to save enough money to send her daughter to Knoxville College in Tennessee. To further her own education, she took night courses at a St. Louis school. By this point she had washed

A laundress washing clothes *(Library of Congress)*

clothes for almost twenty years. Then one day, while scrubbing clothes, she asked herself: "What are you going to do when you grow old and your back gets stiff? This set me to thinking, but with all my thinking I couldn't see how I, a poor washerwoman, was going to better my condition."

She knew of one black woman who had bettered herself. Annie Turnbo (Malone) had moved to St. Louis in 1902 in order to sell the hair-care products she had developed herself. A year later, soon after she had her epiphany that it was time to change her life, Sarah became a Turnbo saleswoman. Sarah had her own problems with hair falling out, which might have been due to scalp disease, poor diet, harmful hair treatments, or stress caused by her volatile marriage.

Annie Turnbo claimed later that she had used her own products on Sarah's scalp and restored her hair. However, Sarah Davis told a different story about her hair restoration. She said it came in a dream:

> A big black man appeared to me and told me what to mix for my hair. Some of the remedy was from Africa, but I sent for it, mixed it, put in on my scalp and in a few weeks my hair was coming in faster than it had ever fallen out. I tried it on my friends; it helped them. I made up my mind I would begin to sell it.

Later, she would use this out-of-Africa story as a great marketing and promotional tool for her products.

In July 1905, Sarah Davis moved to Denver, Colorado, with plans to start her own business marketing African American hair-care products. She was confident she would be a success. She would also be near her sister-in-law and four nieces.

Sarah arrived in Denver with a suitcase and $1.50. She

rented a room in a boardinghouse, where she worked as a cook. She also continued selling Turnbo's products.

Within a few months she had saved enough money to quit her cook's job. She began to experiment with various ingredients, trying the formulas on her own hair and her nieces' hair. She dubbed her first product Wonderful Hair Grower, and claimed it could stop hair loss.

Convinced she was on her way, Sarah cut back her washing to two days a week, and spent the other five making Wonderful Hair Grower and selling it door-to-door. Most of her customers were convinced it helped and told others about it. Sarah was learning that word-of-mouth was a powerful marketing tool.

In January 1906, thirty-eight-year-old Sarah married Charles Joseph Walker, a friend from St. Louis. After her marriage she began to call herself Madam C. J. Walker. She thought it sounded more dignified that Sarah Walker. Her new husband helped her promote her products through advertising in black newspapers and by distributing pamphlets in churches.

Walker decided to open a beauty salon and use her products as treatments. Daughter Lelia, now finished with college, helped with the salon. Walker quit as a Turnbo agent after she began selling her own products, and Annie Turnbo accused her of stealing her ingredients for Wonderful Hair Grower. Competition between the two businesswomen became bitter and personal.

Madam Walker decided to establish her own mail-order business, and in September 1906, the Walkers set off on a year-and-a-half promotional trip to the South. They visited nine states, speaking to black churches and black women's associations. She demonstrated her products, signed up agents, and trained them in her system of hair care.

Back in Denver, Lelia mixed the ingredients, while other family members packed the products and processed orders. Soon the mail-order business began to flourish. Letters poured in from satisfied customers. Texan Julia Coldwell wrote about the benefits of Wonderful Hair Grower, "All the people who know me are just wild about my hair," she said. "I have to take it down to let them see and feel it for themselves. I tell you I am quite an advertisement here for your goods."

Walker thought business opportunities would be greater in a city with a larger black population. In 1908, she decided to move to Pittsburgh, Pennsylvania, where she and her now-married daughter opened a hair-care salon. The city had a black population of almost 25,000, which included lawyers, insurance agents, and twenty-two doctors. Walker reached out to black churches and civic organizations to promote her products.

A year later, Walker and her daughter started Lelia Beauty College in order to train new recruits. They taught the Walker Method, using her Wonderful Hair Grower, Vegetable Shampoo, and Glossine hair oil products. They used a steel comb that was heated to "press" the hair. All graduates received diplomas, certifying them as Walker Hair Culturists.

The new graduates could set up beauty shops in their homes, or they could become agents and sell products door to door. Agents had to sign contracts stating they would sell only Walker products and would use her method of hair treatments in demonstrations. For an extra fee of fifteen dollars, they received a sample kit, which included a steel hair comb with wide prongs, a hairbrush, a scalp comb, and six boxes of Wonderful Hair Grower, Vegetable Shampoo, and Glossine. The saleswomen received a commission, keeping a percentage of their earnings. Black women whose employment had been restricted to domestics or washerwomen now had the opportunity to become independent businesswomen. Walker also benefited from this arrangement. In 1909, her yearly earnings had increased to $8,782, which would be worth more than $200,000 in purchasing power today.

By 1910, she had about one thousand saleswomen in the United States. She traveled constantly, promoting her products and recruiting agents. A dynamic speaker, she gave lectures and demonstrations at churches and women's organizations. Wherever she went, Madam Walker commanded attention. She stood nearly six feet tall, wore fashionable clothes, and had well-groomed hair. She knew that in order to promote her products, she had to promote herself.

However, Madam Walker did not receive welcome from some black men, including Booker T. Washington, who charged that she promoted the looks of white women by straightening hair. Ministers denounced her products in their sermons. Walker countered by saying she did not sell skin bleaches or hair straighteners. "I want the great masses of my people to take greater pride in their appearance," she said, "and to give their hair proper attention." Madam Walker thought her products promoted self-pride and that enhanced appearance gave people a sense of dignity.

In 1910, Walker moved her business to Indianapolis, Indiana, a large shipping center. There she bought a house and set up her hair-care enterprise. In one room, she made up her products, in another she gave beauty treatments. At night,

Booker T. Washington spoke out against the Walker products that could be used to straighten black women's hair. *(Library of Congress)*

she washed clothes. To help with expenses, she rented rooms to boarders and also cooked for them. Her nonstop work paid off. At the end of 1910, Walker's yearly income reached almost $11,000 (which amounts to close to $250,000 in purchasing power today).

The following year, she incorporated her business as the Madam C. J. Walker Manufacturing Company with herself, her daughter, and her husband as board directors. Robert Lee

Brokenburr, a lawyer and former boarder, filed papers for the incorporation of the company. She advertised in black newspapers and magazines. The ads featured "before" and "after" pictures of Walker. The "after" photos showed her with lush, full hair after using her Wonderful Hair Grower.

In addition to Annie Turnbo Malone, Walker faced competition from others in the hair-care business. Black barbers, peddlers, and druggists also made and sold hair-care products. The largest black-owned company in the trade was Overton Hygienic Manufacturing Company. Started by Anthony Overton in 1898 in Kansas City, Kansas, Overton began by producing baking powder. Then Mabel Overton, the owner's daughter, mixed baking powder with cocoa to produce a facial powder for use on darker skin. Sales of "High-Brown" face powder took off, and soon Overton added other toiletries to the line. In 1911, Overton moved his headquarters to Chicago and became the largest black-owned business in the United States. By 1912, Overton had expanded into international markets and grossed sales of about $100,000.

Walker's increasing business success was a result of her ceaseless promotion and smart hiring practices. To manage her day-to-day business while she traveled, Walker selected Freeman B. Ransom, a former boarder and lawyer who graduated from Columbia University in New York. Ransom remained with the company for forty years. She also hired Alice Kelly, an outstanding educator at a teacher-training school. Kelly helped to polish Walker's skills in reading, writing, and etiquette. Walker would later make Kelly forewoman of her Indiana factory.

In July 1912, Walker attended the convention of the National Association of Colored Women (NACW) in

Walker driving her car in 1912 *(Courtesy of New York Public Library)*

Hampton, Virginia. This organization, composed of the most prominent black women of the time, included journalist Ida B. Wells-Barnett, educator Mary McLeod Bethune, and Margaret Murray Washington, wife of Booker T. Washington. The NACW used its considerable influence to address black social and political issues, such as education and racial discrimination. Walker, who had strong opinions about social problems and injustices, gave a stirring speech to the delegates.

A few weeks later, she attended the National Negro Business League (NNBL) convention held in Chicago and

Margaret Murray Washington, wife of Booker T. Washington *(Library of Congress)*

gave her memorable "I-promoted-myself" speech. The convention delegates took notice of this forceful woman. Although Washington had not acknowledged her at the convention, she had got his attention. The following year, he invited Madam Walker to be a featured speaker at the NNBL conference. He introduced her as "one of the most progressive and successful businesswomen of our race . . ." and concluded by saying, "Why, if we don't watch out, the women will excel us."

Although Walker worked hard, she enjoyed the fruits of her labor. She liked beautiful clothes, luxurious furnishing, and automobiles, and she employed a chauffeur. Madam loved music, including hymns and jazz and owned a player organ and a grand piano trimmed with gold. She also enjoyed movies.

In 1912, Madam Walker divorced her husband. They differed on how to run the business. In addition, he squandered money and had affairs with other women. But she gained a new granddaughter when her divorced daughter Lelia Walker Robinson, adopted Fairy Mae Bryant, a thirteen-year-old. The girl had long, braided hair and appeared in Walker advertisements. Walker and her daughter began to groom Mae to eventually take over the business. The teenager accompanied her grandmother on her promotional lectures where she and the Walker nieces set up demonstrations, handed out pamphlets, and signed up agents.

In 1913, Walker decided to expand overseas. She went to Jamaica in November to establish a base of operations in the Caribbean. During the two-month trip, she traveled to Costa Rica, the Panama Canal Zone, Haiti, and Cuba. At each place, she gave demonstrations of her products and urged women to become agents. Soon, throughout the Caribbean, her saleswomen could be seen carrying black valises of Walker products and dressed in a standard outfit: long-sleeved, white starched blouse and black skirt.

Lelia Robinson thought the Walker Company should have a base of operations in both Los Angeles and New York City. She persuaded her mother to buy a four-story town house in West 136th Street in Harlem. The upper floors contained living quarters and a grand meeting salon that became a gathering place for many black writers and performing artists in Harlem. On the floor level, she put in a beauty shop that rivaled the luxurious salons of the white beauty-business entrepreneurs, Helena Rubinstein and Elizabeth Arden. Patrons sat on blue velvet upholstered chairs and sipped tea amidst elegant gray surroundings.

Three years later, Walker moved to Harlem to be near her daughter and granddaughter. Company headquarters remained in Indianapolis with Freeman Ransom in charge. That same year, Walker traveled to the South for another promotional tour. While there, she went back to Mississippi to see her childhood home, and she met with the great-granddaughter of the plantation landowner who had owned her parents as slaves.

The travel began to take a toll on her health. When Walker developed high blood pressure, doctors told her to cut back on her travel and workload and to watch her diet. She went for a two-month rest at Hot Springs, Arkansas, where she took baths in the hot mineral waters. Then, typically, she went on another round of promotional trips.

By 1916, Walker had an estimated 20,000 agents in the United States, the Caribbean, and Central America. In April, she organized her agents into the Madam Walker Hair

Culturists Union of America. The organization protected the rights of the workers and also fostered a sense of togetherness. Agents paid dues of $.25 cents a month. One of the benefits included a $50 payment in case of death. She gave awards to those who had outstanding sales and to those who did community service. One agent wrote, "You have opened up a trade for hundreds of women to make an honest and profitable living, when they make as much in one week as a month's salary would bring from any other position."

The following year, Madam Walker convened her first annual Culturists Union convention in Philadelphia. More than two hundred agents attended. She gave the keynote speech, titled "Women's Duty to Women." In her address, she exhorted her agents to be aggressive in sales. She preached that the women should be role models for other women. She also encouraged them to be active in their communities and involved in political issues.

In the face of growing competition from whites in the cosmetics industry, Walker decided that black cosmetics companies should form a trade organization to protect their markets. In September 1917, she hosted a meeting of a dozen black beauty business leaders at her home. However, she refused to ask Annie Turnbo Malone to attend. The group formed the National Negro Cosmetics Manufacturers Association, with Madam Walker as president. The organization had as its goals to protect their industry against false claims and to help and promote black beauty industry owners.

Madam C. J. Walker began to throw herself into political causes. In July 1917, a race riot occurred in East St. Louis, Illinois. White mobs killed more than three dozen blacks. Walker urged her agents to join in condemning the murders.

She said, "We should protest until the American sense of justice is so aroused, that such affairs as the East St. Louis riot be forever impossible."

To protest the killings, she helped organize a march in New York City. On July 28, 1917, she led the Negro Silent Protest Parade of approximately 15,000 people down Manhattan's Fifth Avenue. Women and children, all dressed in white, led the throng, followed by men in black. They carried signs that said, "Thou Shall Not Kill." Only the sound of marching feet and drum rolls could be heard. Spectators watched in silence.

Madam Walker knew it would take more than speeches and marches to stop the murders. In August, she and other black leaders went to the White House in Washington, D.C., to present a petition to President Woodrow Wilson, asking that lynching be made a federal crime. The president declined to meet with the group, saying he had more pressing matters. The group sent a protest telegram to President Wilson. In spite of this poor treatment, she encouraged blacks to enlist for military service during World War I.

Walker supported and promoted other social causes, particularly education. She gave money to schools and provided scholarships. Her donations went to several institutions, including the Haines Institute in Augusta, Georgia, the Daytona Normal and Industrial Institute for Negro Girls, the Alice Freeman Palmer Memorial Institute in Sedalia, North Carolina, and the Scholarship Fund for Young Women at Tuskegee Institute. She did fund-raising for the National Association for the Advancement of Colored People (NAACP), contributed to the Young Men's Christian Association of Minneapolis, and donated to the preservation of the home of Frederick Douglass in Washington, D.C. Madam Walker said,

"My object in life is not simply to make money for myself or to spend it on myself in dressing or running around in an automobile, but I love to use a part of what I make in trying to help others."

In 1916, Walker bought four-and-a-half acres of land in Irvington-on-Hudson, about twenty miles north of New York City. She hired African American architect Vertner Woodson Tandy, who designed a cream-colored two-story house in an Italian Renaissance style, with sunken gardens and a swimming pool. The house had more than thirty rooms and featured a chapel, poolroom, library, gym, and vaults. Furnishings included marble statues, oil paintings, and Persian rugs. Opera singer Enrico Caruso called it Villa Lewaro. The name came from the first two letters of her daughter's name, <u>Le</u>lia <u>Wa</u>lker <u>Ro</u>binson. Walker moved into her grand house in 1918.

Walker's company continued developing new products. In 1919, it came out with witch hazel, cold cream, cleansing cream, and four shades of face powder. In April, Walker went to St. Louis to promote her new line. While staying with a friend, her health worsened, and she returned to New York, where doctor diagnosed acute kidney failure caused by years of high blood pressure.

The end came fast. Madam C. J. Walker died on May 25, 1919, at the age of fifty-one. According to the doctor attending her, Walker's last words were, "I want to live to help my race."

Her daughter and granddaughter were in Panama and could not get home for the funeral because of travel delays. More than one thousand people attended Walker's funeral, held at Villa Lewaro. Black leaders gave eulogies, praising the work she had done. Madam C. J. Walker was buried at Woodlawn Cemetery in New York.

Villa Lewaro *(Library of Congress)*

In her will, she left her real estate to her daughter Lelia, as well as one-third interest in her company. Two-thirds of the company's net proceeds went to maintenance of Lewaro, to charities, and other black organizations. She also left personal items and money to her employees, friends, and relatives. Finally, she specified that her company remain in the hands of black women. Her daughter assumed the role of president of the company, while Freeman Ransom continued on as manager. In 1927, he expanded the Walker Manufacturing

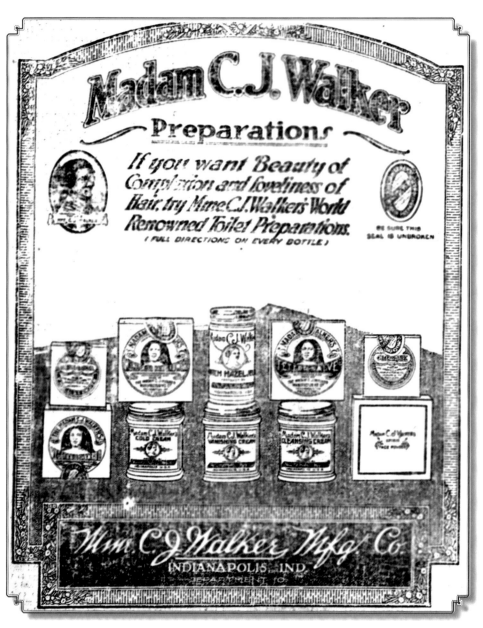

A 1920 advertisement for Walker's line of beauty products *(Library of Congress)*

Company into a million-dollar complex, which included offices, manufacturing, and a community center.

When Walker's beloved daughter died in 1931, her grand-daughter became president of the company. When Mae died, her daughter inherited the company stock and served as its head. The company still sells some products today, although it no longer remains in family hands. Walker's former head-quarters in Indianapolis and her home Villa Lewaro are listed as National Historical Landmarks.

Madam C. J. Walker took pride in the company she built, but she took greater pride in helping to provide opportunities for black women. "I promoted myself," she said. "I had to make my own living and my own opportunity. But I did it! Don't sit down and wait for opportunities to come . . . Get up and make them!"

Madam C. J. Walker timeline

1867   Born as Sarah Breedlove in Delta, Louisiana, on December 23.

1874   Orphaned.

1878   Moves with sister to Vicksburg, Mississippi.

1882   Marries Moses McWilliams, who dies in 1888.

1885   Daughter Lelia is born.

1889   Moves to St. Louis, Missouri.

1894   Marries John Davis; couple separates in 1903.

1905   Moves to Denver, Colorado.

1905   Develops hair-care formula for black women.

1906   Marries Charles Joseph Walker.

1908   Opens an office in Pittsburgh; establishes Lelia College.

1910   Moves headquarters to Indianapolis, Indiana.

1911 Establishes the Madam C. J. Walker Manufacturing Company.

1912 Divorces Charles Walker.

1913 Expands her market to the Caribbean and Central America.

1916 Moves to New York City.

1917- 1918 Builds Villa Lewaro in Irvington-on-Hudson, New York.

1919 Dies at her home, on May 25; buried in New York City.

FIVE

Helena Rubinstein

Inspiration often comes from unlikely places. For Helena Rubinstein, it happened in Coleraine, a small town in the Australian outback when she arrived there in 1896 to stay with her uncle and cousin. Among other personal items, she carried twelve jars of her mother's cold cream. She noticed that the Australian women had sunburned and rough complexions. "My own skin was soft and fresh and remained so even in that terrible climate. First one woman was asking to use it [the cream] and then another and I wrote home asking that supplies be sent to me by the first boat," she later said. The twenty-four-year-old suddenly realized that her creams could help other women have smoother skin—and she could make money bringing that cream to them. She called the cream her "fingers of fate."

Helena Rubinstein was born on Christmas Day, sometime between 1870 and 1872 in Krakow, Poland. Her parents, Gitel and Hertzel Rubinstein, named their firstborn daughter Chaja. She learned to assume responsibility at a young age. Not only did she have charge of her seven younger sisters at home, she also helped with bookkeeping at her father's hardware store. She attended school until the age of fifteen or sixteen.

Around the age of sixteen, Chaja fell in love with a student at the university but her father objected to the relationship and arranged for her to marry an older man. The headstrong daughter rebelled, quarreling so much with her family that they ordered her out of the house. She did not marry the student, but during the next few years she lived with maternal aunts.

In her mid-twenties, Chaja emigrated to Australia. On the passage over, she listed her age as twenty and gave her name as Helena. After Rubinstein arrived in Coleraine, she helped her cousin with her three children, and worked in her uncle's general store. She also attended the local public school to learn English.

When Rubinstein began selling her creams in the general store it caused conflict with her uncle. She spent three unhappy years in Coleraine before she could escape. "I had to get to Melbourne," she said, "to a metropolis, where I felt there would be more scope for my ideas and energies. . . . I took things in my own hands."

Rubinstein did not yet have enough money to start her own business. She moved to Queensland, Australia, and worked as a nanny. After three years, she moved on to Melbourne, where she labored as a waitress and a nanny. There she finally found people who could help her realize her dream. John Thompson, manager of an import company, taught her how to market her products. From Frederick Grimwade, chairman of a pharmaceutical company, she learned about cream

A photo of Rubinstein from around the time she started her business
(*Courtesy of AP Images*)

formulas and how to mix them. She developed a passion for working in the laboratory and later said she spent her happiest moments in her "kitchens."

In 1903, Rubinstein opened a beauty salon in downtown Melbourne. It is unclear who provided the money for her business venture. She called it Maison de Beautè Valaze, "House of Beauty Valaze," the name of her beauty cream. She painted the front rooms white and added rattan furniture. In the back room, she mixed her creams and packaged them in jars bearing gold, black, and ginger-colored labels. In the local newspapers, she advertised her cream Valaze as "skin food." At first, women came into the shop out of curiosity. The salon owner personally demonstrated how to use the cream, massaging the emollient upward on the neck and face. The recipients usually bought jars to take home.

While giving her facial demonstrations, Rubinstein discovered that different skin types—dry, oily, normal, and others—needed different types of creams. She adjusted her formula and became the first skin culturist to offer specific creams for specific skin types. Soon, she expanded her range of products, adding cleansing creams, astringents, and medicated soaps. She worked almost constantly, and saved her money.

A woman journalist from Sydney, Australia, heard about Helena Rubinstein and came to interview her. The salon owner showed the writer how to apply the cream and gave her a free jar. The journalist wrote a favorable article in the Sydney newspaper, extolling the benefits of the cream Valaze. Women flocked to the salon. So many mail orders poured in from all over Australia that she had trouble keeping up with the demand. The article was the beginning of a lifelong admiration and appreciation that Rubinstein had for the printed media.

In 1905, Rubinstein returned to Europe and spent a few weeks in London, scouting out possible locations for a salon. She also spent time going to health spas, a tradition among Europeans. There she took treatments in the mineral waters and visited clinics where she studied the latest in skin therapy. During her European trip, Rubinstein went to visit her family in Krakow. It was the last time she ever saw her parents. She did take her sister Ceska and her daughter back to Australia to help her with the booming business.

In 1906, she met Edward Titus, a Polish-born journalist who held a U.S. passport. They married two years later, in London, and Titus would prove to be a valuable asset. Rubinstein hired Titus to write and edit copy for her advertisements. Before long he was handling all of her advertising. He helped with product designs and with her Sydney salon and encouraged her ambitious expansion plans, which included opening beauty salons in Europe. Helena Rubinstein was determined to become the first woman to establish a global business.

In 1908, the entrepreneur opened her elegant salon in London, England. She painted the shop in bright, bold colors. To drum up business, she gave free skin treatments to a few influential women. She understood that favorable word-of-mouth advertising would bring in more customers. By the end of her first year, Rubinstein had one thousand regular clients. She had become a wealthy woman.

Rubinstein had always enjoyed the theater, and she began to experiment with makeup she saw on the stage. Actress Gabrielle Ray showed her how to shade color on the skin and how to use eye shadow to highlight the eyes. She also taught her how to apply makeup to hide defects. Rubinstein soon added rouges to her line. Because of societal disapproval of "painted faces" and fear of being seen, patrons entered her salon through a side door. Before long, however, they were coming through the front door.

In 1909, Rubinstein opened a salon in Paris. That same year, she gave birth to her first son Roy. Three years later, at the age of forty, she gave birth to her second son, Horace.

Actress Gabrielle Ray showed Rubinstein cosmetic techniques used by stage actors. *(Library of Congress)*

A 1921 advertisement for Valaze *(Courtesy of Mary Evans Picture Library/Alamy)*

Motherhood did not slow her down, however. She began studying dermatology at St. Louis Hospital in Paris and turned management of her Paris salon over to her sister Pauline.

During this time, Rubinstein became a serious art collector, particularly of modern paintings. This new, edgy art fit her tastes and provided inspiration for many of her product designs. Rubinstein also started to purchase artifacts from Africa, eventually gathering one of the most important African art collections in the world. Whether collecting art works or selecting her products, she always trusted her "inner eye."

In October 1914, Rubinstein left for the United States in search of more business opportunities. Her husband and two small sons followed about six months later. When she arrived in New York she saw women wearing rice powder. "Here is not only a new country," she said, "but a huge new market for my products." She wanted to reach a larger buying audience beyond the salon and decided to first develop a wholesale business and sell her products to retail stores. But she wanted only the best retail stores to carry her name brand. She visited large cities across the United States to check out fine, established department stores, and trained store employees on how to demonstrate and sell her products. To make sure her goods were displayed and properly sold, she often stood behind the counter herself.

In May 1915, Helena Rubinstein opened a grand salon on New York's East Forty-Ninth Street. It created a sensation. The press raved about the interior walls covered with dark blue velvet, the light-blue silk furnishings, and the striking sculptures created by Polish artist Elie Nadelman. *Vogue* magazine ran a gushing column about Rubinstein's new business. Like the openings of her earlier shops, Rubinstein's New

York salon proved to be a success. Ten years later, she would move her salon to prestigious Fifth Avenue.

It did not deter Rubinstein that she faced another established competitor in New York. Elizabeth Arden, a Canadian immigrant, had opened her salon in 1908 and targeted the same privileged clientele. Rubinstein and Arden tried to outdo each other in new products and in advertising, and even hired away each other's employees. A lifelong animosity developed between them, although they never met personally.

Rubinstein worked sixteen to eighteen hours a day, and it took a toll on her already shaky marriage. Her husband complained about her long absences. By 1916, she and Edward Titus had separated, and he returned to Europe where he opened a bookstore. Her husband remained a shareholder in the company and continued to write advertising copy. He also scouted out properties in Europe for her. The boys remained with their mother.

Rubinstein continued to expand her business. By 1917, she had established salons in Boston, Philadelphia, and San Francisco. That same year, she built a manufacturing plant on Long Island, New York, one year before Arden opened her own plant. She opened a staff training school in New York and expanded her wholesale market to include more department stores. She wanted her products to maintain their elite aura, and yet to be bought by shop and office workers.

During the 1920s, Helena Rubinstein built one of the most successful cosmetics businesses in the United States. So it came as a surprise when, in 1928, she sold her American firm to Lehman Brothers, an investment company. When Lehman started selling her products in variety stores, she was horrified that her name products would be placed in stores that sold cheap goods. She asked the women stockholders to pressure Lehman to sell the company back to her, saying men did not understand the beauty needs of women. When the stock market crashed in 1929, Rubinstein bought back enough stock to gain control of the company—at a fraction of what she had sold for. By 1931, she had her company back, and had made a nice profit. Now sixty, Rubinstein went back to work in her New York office.

Rubinstein employed most of her family in her business at one point. She put her sisters, nieces, and cousins in charge of her European and Australian subsidiaries and brought her grown sons into the company. Roy became chairman of the board, and Horace was appointed creative director. However, Rubinstein depended most on her niece Mala Rubinstein Silson, also a creative director, and her nephew Oscar Kolin, executive vice-president of the company.

By all accounts, Rubinstein set high standards for herself, and she expected the same of her employees. If she did not like a staff member, she had the employee's desk moved out before she arrived for work the next morning. Patrick O'Higgins, her personal assistant, recalled that, "Madame liked the feeling of activity around her. She enjoyed the confusion, and, even if fully occupied, she kept her office door open so as to monitor traffic outside, through the corner of one eye."

Rubinstein kept tight control over expenses and was always conscious of operating costs. She seldom gave raises, or benefits, to her workers, except those hired away from Elizabeth Arden. Periodically, she prowled the office building, turning off lights and muttering how expensive electricity was. She fished paper out of wastebaskets and wondered why people did not use both sides of the sheet before throwing it away.

She always carried her lunch in a brown paper bag and ate at her desk. However, she entertained at the best restaurants when she had a new business client or was wooing a member of the media.

If Rubinstein had problems with employees, she excelled in her relations with the press. She had as great an instinct for public relations as she did for cosmetics. When she had a new product to launch, she invited magazine editors to her home and showed off her latest acquisitions of art and jewelry. If an editor admired some bauble she wore, Madame took it off and gave it to her—but she never gave away her finest jewelry. She wanted to make sure she would get lead articles in fashion magazines, and usually did. Articles and editorials brought in more sales than ads she thought, and did not cost anything.

Twice yearly, Rubinstein traveled to Europe, where she checked on her subsidiaries and properties. She also went to health spas to take treatments for phlebitis and other circulatory problems, which plagued her all her life. When she traveled on the train, she booked coach class and carried her food in brown paper bags. She sat with her feet propped on her vanity case filled with jewels. On her trips, Rubinstein spent large sums of money buying clothes, jewelry, and art. "I owe it to the business," she said.

During the 1920s and 1930s, makeup became more popular with American women, largely due to Rubinstein's and Arden's efforts to make cosmetics respectable. A suntan craze swept the country and women took henna baths to darken their skins. Rubinstein added sunscreen to her line, and brought out lotions that smoothed on instant tans. "Sunburn is beauty suicide," she said at one point. She experimented with a mascara that would not run when wet. In 1939, she introduced the first waterproof mascara and it became her most famous product.

But the cosmetics industry also experienced a backlash. The American Medical Association expressed concern about allergic reactions to beauty products. Most allergies to cosmetics were—and are—due to the preservatives or fragrances added to the products. In 1934, M. C. Phillips wrote a book called *Skin Deep,* and promoted it as an exposé on cosmetics contents. The criticisms had merit. One company made a depilatory named Koremlu that contained rat poison. Another made an eye makeup called Lash Lure that contained aniline dye, which could cause blindness. First Lady Eleanor Roosevelt and other women's groups, such as the League of Women Voters, clamored for reform of the beauty business.

The cosmetics industry leaders, including Rubinstein, fought restrictions on their products. In 1938, Congress passed the Food, Drug, and Cosmetics Act, which imposed controls on the labeling and advertising claims of cosmetic manufacturers. The Federal Food and Drug Administration (FDA) told Rubinstein that she could not advertise her Valaze as skin food, so she renamed it Novena Cerate, or night cream. She began advertising other creams to be used for different times of the day—a first in the cosmetics industry. "Take advantage of the situation," she always said. "Every situation!"

Rubinstein had several ways to deal with the stress caused by problems. She took long walks and wrote letters to friends, shopped, had her portrait painted (more than thirty during her lifetime), and there was always work. "It keeps the wrinkles out of the mind and the spirit," she said. However, during a real crisis, she fled or withdrew, usually into her bedroom

First Lady Eleanor Roosevelt campaigned for more safety regulations in the cosmetics industry. *(Library of Congress)*

until she could find a strategy for coping, or she left for a business trip.

In 1937, Rubinstein divorced Edward Titus. A year later, she married Prince Artchil Gourielli-Tchkonia, rumored to be from a noble family in pre-revolutionary Russia. Madame Rubinstein reveled in the title of princess. Her new husband was more than twenty years younger, and possessed wit and charm. He also did not require much attention—and he did not interfere with her business. A decade later, she developed a skin-care line for men called House of Gourielli. She also opened a separate men's salon on East Fifty-fifth Street. But the Gourielli line and the salon failed. Her ideas for men beauty products were ahead of their time.

In 1941, Rubinstein came out with a fragrance called Heaven Scent. To launch the new product she packaged it in a blue bottle shaped like an angel. She put miniature bottles of her new fragrance in decorated baskets and floated them with pink and blue balloons over Fifth Avenue. Each basket

Rubinstein conducts a makeup class in 1945 *(Courtesy of Hulton Archive/ Getty Images)*

Rubinstein in her laboratory in 1940 *(Courtesy of Lipnitzki/Roger Viollet/Getty Images)*

contained a card saying, "A gift for you from Heaven! Helena Rubinstein's 'Heaven Scent.'" "Good publicity doesn't need too many facts," was on of her favorite sayings.

During World War II, the Nazis seized most of Rubinstein's salons and factories in Europe. Her American subsidiaries remained open, although production was curtailed due to restrictions on raw products used in cosmetics.

Rubinstein helped in the war effort by opening beauty salons in armament factories where many women now worked, and she conducted fund-raising for the Red Cross. The United States War Department commissioned Rubinstein to make supply kits for troops in "Operation Torch," the huge Allied military campaign in North Africa. Her company produced 60,000 kits that contained sunburn cream, camouflage makeup, and skin cleaner. When the war ended in 1945, Rubinstein reopened her shops in Paris and refurbished the London salon.

By the 1950s, Helena Rubinstein faced competition on many fronts. Not only was Elizabeth Arden going strong, but Charles Revson had made Revlon into one of the largest cosmetics companies in the world (The "l" in Revlon stands for Charles Lachman, an original partner). It was so successful that Rubinstein secretly bought stocks of Revlon. A small company named Estée Lauder attracted customers when it came out with a wildly popular fragrance. As a result of the increased competition, Rubinstein's sales began to lag. In response, she redid old products, repackaged them, and sold them as new and different. She launched a new men's line, but it did not do well.

In November 1955, while Rubinstein was in Paris, her husband, Prince Gourielli, died of a heart attack in New York. She took to her bed and ordered flowers sent, but she did not attend the funeral, citing ill health and pressing business.

She continued to travel. In 1957, she made a world tour of her businesses in Asia, Australia, and New Zealand. It had been thirty years since she had last visited Australia, and she received the attention of a queen and gloried in the media coverage.

In 1959, her youngest son Horace died of a heart attack following an automobile crash. When she received news of

Horace's death, Helena Rubinstein crawled into bed, pulled the covers over her head, and wept for her child. Although she often quarreled with him, Rubinstein loved her son, and she berated herself for not having been a better mother. A few years earlier Horace had suggested creating a foundation bearing her name. The foundation, created in 1953, gave money to her favorite cultural projects, and even better, the funds remained tax-exempt. After her son's death, she went to Israel and established an art pavilion in Tel Aviv.

In the 1960s, treatment creams with hormones and vitamins became popular and Rubinstein brought out a hormone-based cream. She also developed the mascara wand, which rolled the mascara onto the eyelashes. She continued to make her twice-yearly business trips to Europe, although she now had to take a nurse with her, in addition to her personal assistant. In New York, she made her weekly visits to her factory, and she went to her New York office every day; she could not fathom why her employees needed vacations.

Although Rubinstein felt the effects of old age, she still remained a formidable figure. One morning in May 1964, she had her usual breakfast in bed when three masked and armed robbers burst into her bedroom, demanding the keys to her safe and her locked cabinets. Rubinstein said, "I'm an old woman. Death doesn't frighten me. You can kill me, but you can't rob me—now get out." As they rummaged through drawers, she slipped the keys from her purse and hid them under the folds of the covers. The robbers dragged her out of bed and tied her to a chair but she shrieked and thrashed about until the thieves fled—with only $200 they found in her purse.

On March 31, 1965, while at work, Rubinstein experienced a minor stroke. An ambulance rushed her to a New

York hospital where she suffered a massive stroke during the night. On April 1, Helena Rubinstein died—alone. Her obituary in the *New York Times* gave her age as ninety-four. The paper noted that at the time of her death, she had 30,000 employees in more than one hundred countries. Her personal estate was estimated to be worth more than $100 million.

In her will, she left money to her family but tied it up in trusts. She gave paltry amounts to her domestic staff who had served her faithfully for many years. She left her best pieces of jewelry to her sisters and nieces.

Rubinstein specified that the remainder of her jewels and most of her art collection be auctioned off. The proceeds went to the Helena Rubinstein Foundation, as did a large number of stocks in her company.

Helena Rubinstein wanted her company and brand to exist for a long time. "I want the business to last three hundred years," she said. This was a grand vision, and one that might very well come true.

Helena Rubinstein timeline

1870-
1872(?) Born in Krakow, Poland, on December 25.

1896   Emigrates to Australia.

1903   Opens beauty salon in Melbourne, Australia.

1908   Opens beauty shop in London; marries Edward Titus.

1909   Son Roy is born; opens salon in Paris, France.

1912   Son Horace is born.

1914   Immigrates to the United States.

1915   Opens salon in New York City.

1917   Builds a manufacturing plant on Long Island, New York.

1928   Sells New York firm to Lehman Brothers.

1929-
1931   Buys back her New York firm.

1937   Divorces Edward Titus.

1938	Marries Prince Artchil Gourielli-Tchkonia.
1939	Develops the first waterproof mascara.
1953	Establishes the Helena Rubinstein Foundation.
1955	Prince Gourielli dies.
1959	Horace Titus dies; opens Helena Rubinstein Art Pavilion in Tel Aviv, Israel.
1965	Dies in New York City, on April 1.

SIX

Elizabeth Arden

Beauty queen Elizabeth Arden always lined her expensive shoes with newspaper. She began doing this as a child when, as the daughter of an impoverished tenant farmer, she needed it to keep out the wet and cold. Because she grew up with few material goods, she became determined not to remain poor and told her siblings, "I want to be the richest little woman in the world."

As an adult, Elizabeth Arden, born Florence Nightingale Graham, never talked much about her early life. No one knew exactly when she was born, though dates range from 1878 to 1884. According to one biographer, her birth records show she was born December 31, 1881, in Woodbridge, Ontario, north of Toronto, Canada. Her mother Susan named her for the famous nurse and Red Cross founder. A pretty child, Florence had auburn hair, blue eyes, and beautiful skin, which she inherited from her mother. She had two older sisters,

Christine and Lillian, one brother Willie, and one younger sister, Gladys. Their father William sold vegetables grown on his rented plot of ground. He also peddled household supplies to other farmers in the area.

When Florence was about six, her mother died of tuberculosis and she and her three older siblings had to assume most of their mother's chores. Florence had the best organizational skills in the family and gradually became the manager of the household. Her father also made her responsible for the care of the horses—feeding, watering, grooming, and exercising them. She drove the horses while he peddled his goods and to earn extra money she raised flowers and sold them at the village market. Flowers remained her lifelong passion.

Florence Graham had no chance to go to college, a fact she always lamented. At the age of seventeen, she went into nurses training in Toronto but soon discovered she could not stand the sight of blood and didn't like to look at sick people. She did enjoy visiting the hospital laboratory, where she watched a biochemist develop creams for skin disorders.

When she returned home, Graham had the idea of making creams for her own mail-order business. She experimented with making a facial cream on her wood stove. The stench drove her family out of the house and prompted neighbors to bring in food because they thought the Grahams had been reduced to eating rotten eggs.

Soon her father gave his daughter an ultimatum: either get married or find work. She headed back to Toronto. Over the next few years, she worked as a bank teller, a secretary, and a dental receptionist. She also kept the dentist's accounts and discovered he had a declining business. Graham sent all his patients a letter, describing the horrible effects on their gums and teeth if they did not get to the dentist.

In 1907, Graham left Canada to follow her brother Willie to New York City. There she worked first as a bookkeeper with E. R. Squibb and Sons, a pharmaceutical company. The following year, she found employment as a cashier in a beauty parlor. The owner, Eleanor Adair, had a fashionable salon where she used a head strapping device and her own creams that supposedly tightened the face and neck muscles. Graham persuaded the owner to teach her how to give facial treatments and how to massage skin. She spent a year with Adair, learning about creams and giving manicures and massages. She became good at her new trade.

In 1909, Florence Graham met Elizabeth Hubbard, another ambitious woman. Hubbard wanted to open a salon featuring her own skin preparations. The two women formed a business partnership and opened their New York shop at 509 Fifth Avenue and Forty-second Street. The salon, bearing Elizabeth Hubbard's name, was located near the fine shops and restaurants frequented by the well-to-do. Graham was thrilled about the prestigious address, but the strong-willed owners argued about everything and the partnership dissolved in six months. Hubbard took her creams and moved two doors down to open her own salon.

Nearing thirty, Florence Graham decided to go into business making and selling her own creams. Where she got her start-up money is unclear. Some sources say that either her brother or her uncle provided the capital; others believe she borrowed money from a bank.

Graham decided that she wanted a different name. She did not deem her birth name sophisticated enough for her establishment. She kept Florence N. Graham as her legal name but liked the sound of Elizabeth and decided to use it. Accounts differ on how she arrived at her last name. Some sources say she picked it from Alfred Lloyd Tennyson's poem, "Enoch Arde," others said it came from the name of a famous country estate in upper New York. Elizabeth Arden sounded high-class, and that was what mattered to her.

Arden stood five feet two inches tall and walked with a listing gait, caused by a hip injury in her youth. (While dancing the cancan, she had thrown her hip out of joint during a high kick.) She was nearsighted, but did not like to wear glasses and became one of the first women to wear contact lenses. Her impairments never slowed her down; she always kept in motion. Arden ate sparingly and wore a size ten or twelve all her life. With her trim figure and flawless skin she looked fifteen to twenty years younger than her actual age.

In 1910, she opened her salon at the same Fifth Avenue address, with her new name now on the shop. To help pay the rent, Arden sublet one room to two successful hairdressers, the Ogilvie sisters. Women could have their skin and hair done at the same place, a novel beauty-business concept at the time. Arden kept the front room for her salon and decorated it in soft colors and antiques. She spent so much on decor that she could not afford a cleaning woman, so she cleaned it herself. Finally, she added one more detail: she painted her outside door a bright red. It became as recognizable a trademark as her name.

During the day, Arden gave skin treatments and massages. At night, she made up her creams in the back room. She packaged her emollients in pink and gold-labeled jars tied with pink ribbons. She labeled her creams "Venetian," continuing her

A cosmetic class at an Elizabeth Arden salon *(Courtesy of Ralph Crane/Time Life Pictures/Getty Images)*

commitment to promoting her products as classy and desirable. As her customers increased, she added a receptionist and trained carefully selected young women how to sell and to give facial massages. She called them her "treatment girls." Years later, the Ogilvie sisters would say about Elizabeth Arden, "the way she could sell! And the way she could train other girls to sell—it was astonishing!" Hubbard could not match her competitor and closed her shop within two years.

From the beginning, Elizabeth Arden targeted an upper-class clientele. She followed the activities of the rich and socially prominent women of the time—the Astors, Vanderbilts, and Whitneys. She longed to become part of that society and hid her lower-class background. She took speech lessons so that her voice sounded soft and whispery, read etiquette books, and mimicked the manners of the well-to-do. She dressed in beautiful clothes and had the finest of furnishings. Her desire to be accepted into that wealthy society increased her ambition.

Arden realized the importance of advertising and poured her profits back into marketing. She advertised in *Vogue* and other leading women's magazines and hired the best photographers and illustrators to do her ads. She was particularly picky about the wording in her ads and often wrote her own copy, and continued to even after she could afford high-powered advertising agencies. Wealthy women, attracted by her beautifully packaged products and her advertisements, flocked into Arden's shop.

Arden began to tint her facial powders and experimented with rouges, practices not widely used in the United States at that time. At the beginning of the twentieth century, a woman's beauty routine remained fairly simple. Her skin treatment consisted of washing her face and smoothing on oil or cream. She plucked her eyebrows, dusted her face with rice powder, and rubbed balm on her lips. To add color to her face, she pinched her cheeks. Most American women did not wear colored makeup; painted faces were associated with prostitutes and stage actresses.

In 1912, Arden went to Paris to gather new ideas for her business. She claimed she made a tour of all the salons in the city. At each, she took skin treatments, and if she could not talk the sales women into giving her free samples, she bought their products. Arden noticed something women did not do in America. Parisian women wore eye makeup. In the United States, only women on the stage or "women on the street" accented their eyes. When Arden returned to her New York salon, she began applying eye shadow and mascara on some of her socially prominent—and daring—clients, promising to give them their money back if they did not attract attention. Soon, other women began asking for eye makeup. Arden never had to give a refund.

On her return voyage from France to the United States, she found something else that attracted her—a gentleman by the name of Thomas Jenkins Lewis. A silk salesman, Lewis was as smooth and elegant as the goods he sold. He had a charming disposition and a gift for conversation, attractive attributes in Arden's mind. During the journey, the couple dined and talked and danced. Lewis asked his attractive, energetic companion to marry him, but she declined. Elizabeth Arden had more important things on her mind.

Back in the United States, she met with A. Fabian Swanson, a chemist at a pharmaceutical firm and asked him to develop new products for her business. He developed a whipped face cream that she called Venetian Amoretta, and Ardena Skin Tonic, a mild astringent. Both became best sellers. Swanson would prove to be one of the most fortunate finds of Arden's career. The two formed a business partnership in 1915 and worked together for more than forty years.

By 1914, Arden decided to expand her business. She opened her first branch salon in Washington, D.C, and it was successful immediately. She also began selling her products wholesale to specialty shops and the most upscale department stores. This was immensely profitable. She paid on average about three cents for the raw ingredients in a jar that sold for $2.50. After deducting all of her expenses she made about sixty cents on a jar—a 25 percent profit.

On November 29, 1915, Elizabeth Arden finally married Thomas Lewis. The day of the wedding she worked at her salon until 4:00 PM, took off an hour for the ceremony, came back at 5:00, worked until 8:00, and then joined her new husband for a wedding supper. She hired him to handle the wholesale side of her business, but never offered him a business partnership nor gave him stock in the company. Lewis proved to be a brilliant salesman and greatly expanded her sales markets to retail stores. Arden hired her brother Willie to assist him.

Helena Rubinstein (*Courtesy of Hulton Archive/Getty Images*)

In 1915, Helena Rubinstein, who had already established her beauty empire in Australia and Europe, opened her first American salon on Fifth Avenue, targeting the same moneyed clients Arden had cultivated.

Arden now faced her first serious competition, and she did not like it. Building a bigger cosmetics empire than Rubinstein became her lifelong obsession. She never referred to her rival by her name, instead calling her "that dreadful woman." During their long careers, the two women regularly hired each other's employees and despised one another, although they never personally met.

During the 1920s, a social and cultural revolution occurred in the United States. Women gained the right to vote and began to seek employment outside the home. Advertising and consumption of goods accelerated. Women, particularly in the bigger cities, threw away their binding corsets and wore loose-fitting clothes and bobbed their hair. The decade became known as the Age of the Flapper—the new, freed woman. The flappers demanded makeup, and the beauty queens gave them what they wanted.

Arden wanted to expand her business to international markets. In October 1922, she opened a London salon on Bond Street. She hired Edward Haslam, a superb manager, to run her London business. Her sister Gladys, who spoke impeccable French, talked Elizabeth into letting her open a salon in Paris. Gladys ran the Elizabeth Arden branch in France until her death. She tirelessly promoted her sister's products, and the business grew profitable. Gladys passed along clever packaging ideas to her sister and even sent a perfumer to develop new scents.

Arden also opened salons in Rome, Italy, and Berlin, Germany. All had prestigious locations, elegant interiors, and bright red doors. Before the decade ended, Thomas Lewis expanded Arden's products to stores in Asia, Australia, Africa, and South America. By 1925, Arden had established salons in Los Angeles, San Francisco, Boston, Philadelphia, Newport, and Palm Beach, Florida.

After a flare-up of her old hip injury, she decided to try yoga instead of surgery. Arden became convinced of the benefits of physical fitness, so she added exercise rooms to her salons. She often led dance lessons or a yoga class, and surprised people with her ability to stand on her head, even well into her seventies.

Elizabeth Arden also introduced a number of other innovations. She developed the first travel-sized beauty products and launched the first newsletter in the cosmetics industry. She invited women to write to her about their skin problems, and of course, responded with recommendations for her products. "Every woman has the right to be beautiful," she said. "And with my help, they will achieve their rights."

Elizabeth Arden had a simple business philosophy: make quality products and do everything possible to promote and sell them. She believed that in order to make money, one had to spend money. She spent a fortune in advertising and continued to add more products. Toward the end of the 1920s, Arden offered more than seventy-five individual items. She launched four fragrances in 1929 alone. Her wholesale business to department stores amounted to $2 million a year.

Arden set certain criteria in choosing people to work for her. She would not hire anyone who wore glasses or sported beards, all her employees had to be good-looking, and she did not like her male executives to be married. She fired those employees she caught smoking or wearing brown. As arbitrary as they seemed, most of her requirements had to do with maintaining image and made perfect sense to her.

Arden paid her people well. Her salesmen made up to $17,000 a year, and "treatment girls" earned $60 a week, plus tips. At the time an average garment worker made about $18 a week. But in return she demanded total loyalty and called staff members at all hours. She also expected perfection and chastised employees when something went wrong. One staff member stopped at church every morning to pray that she would not make a mistake at work that day. Employees at her salons panicked when they heard she was coming. "I don't want them to love me," Arden said. "I want them to fear me."

Her highly paid, talented executives did not fare much better. During business meetings, she would ask opinions from her male executives and then would totally disregard their suggestions—it was her means of establishing who had control. Arden hated to delegate authority and micromanaged everything. Those employees who remained with her learned how to cope and ignore her demands. One staff member told a new hire, "It's easy. There's only one thing you have to know about Miss Arden. If she says come—you come. If she says go—you go."

Elizabeth Arden's signature color was pink, ranging from deep cherry to lavender. She thought pink to be the most flattering of all colors, and she used it everywhere. She wore pink clothing and splashed her homes with pink, including rich displays of flowers. There were pink cashmere car floor mats and she sent her press releases out on pink paper. She had seventy-five shades of pink in her line of products and she could tell the difference between all of them.

By the 1930s, the economic boom had collapsed into the Great Depression. Millions lost their job and families went hungry. However, Arden's wealthy customers could still afford to buy her expensive products; therefore, she did not worry about the terrible economic state of the nation. In 1932, she wrote in *Ladies' Home Journal* an encouragement for the women of America to smile, and assured them that financial crisis was nearing its end.

Arden certainly knew how to live well. In addition to her Fifth Avenue penthouse, she bought an estate in Mount Vernon, Maine, she called Maine Chance, where she and her husband had a constant string of weekend guests they entertained. They seemed to be a golden couple, but under the

surface the marriage had long before unraveled. When Lewis
tried to alienate his wife from some of her staff members, she
fired him. He had several affairs with other women, which
she decided to overlook, but would not tolerate being under-
mined in her business. She divorced Thomas Lewis in 1934.
Her brother Willie sided with her husband in the bitter split,
so she fired him as well. She never spoke Willie's name again,
but remained close to his three daughters. Her niece, Patricia
Young, later became her constant companion.

Elizabeth Arden threw herself into her work and launched
one of her most ambitious projects. She decided to build a spa
resort on her Maine Chance property. In 1934, she opened

Arden examines cosmetic samples at her desk in 1936. *(Courtesy of Alfred
Eisenstaedt/Time & Life Pictures/Getty Images)*

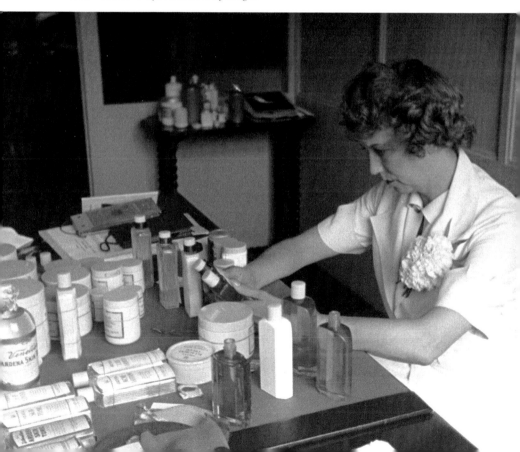

the first luxury health spa in the United States. It had finely furnished guest cottages for the twenty women who stayed each week. The Maine spa center featured exercise rooms, steam rooms, dance and fencing studios, and beauty treatment rooms. It also had a large swimming pool where butlers delivered fruit drinks in silver goblets to lounging guests. In the dining room, a chef offered "light' meals during the day which concluded with a formal dinner in the evening. Guests had breakfast in bed, served on bone china with a fresh rose on the tray. Arden hired a staff of forty people to cater to her clientele. For this attention and pampering, women paid more than $500 a week. She would later add a winter spa in Phoenix, Arizona.

During the 1930s, Arden found her other great passion in life. A friend said she needed a hobby and suggested horse racing. She bought her first horse in 1931 and threw almost as much money, energy, and ambition into horse racing as she did her business. "My business is to make women beautiful," she said. "My sport is to raise beautiful horses." Arden stabled her horses at Maine Chance, but she also bought horse farms in South Carolina and Kentucky. In racing she went by the name Mrs. Elizabeth N. Graham. Jockeys wore her racing colors of white, blue, and cerise (cherry red). She demanded as much from her jockeys and trainers as she did from her business employees, saying "you've got to fight, fight, fight!"

Arden truly loved horses and spared no time and expense on their care. She had soothing music piped into their stalls and plants hung overhead. After every race, she directed the staff to rub down the horses with Ardena Skin Tonic Lotion and wash with her fragrance Blue Grass. She had the stable hands massage the horses' legs with her Eight Hour Cream and had the animals draped in pink cashmere blankets. Arden carried pictures of her horses in her billfold and showed them off like a proud mother would her children.

In the 1940s, when she was in her sixties, Elizabeth Arden experienced some setbacks. Always interested in films, she produced the movie *Young and Beautiful* and lost money on it. She married again in 1942, to Russian "Prince" Michael Evlanoff, who was seventeen years younger. Following the marriage, Arden insisted that her staff address her as "Princess." Although an entertaining escort, Evlanoff proved to be a poor choice for a husband. He idled his time away and he spent her money. The marriage lasted about a year.

During the 1930s, World War II began raging across Europe. Arden began stockpiling raw materials such as oil and alcohol. Her company continued to manufacture her products until the United States entered the war in December 1941. As a morale booster, the War Department commissioned Arden to provide makeup kits for the U.S. Marine Corps Women's Reserve. The kits contained rouge, matching lipstick and nail polish, which she named "Montezuma Red." Arden also sponsored other war efforts, such as fundraisers for the Red Cross. She had her London chemists develop a cream to heal terrible burn scars suffered by troops in combat and had the cream distributed to hospitals that treated children and other patients disfigured from facial burns.

Elizabeth Arden did have one big worry during World War II. Her sister Gladys, who remained in Paris, publicly criticized the Nazi occupation of France and helped downed Allied pilots escape. The Nazis responded by shipping her to a concentration camp in northern Germany. Gladys' aristocratic French husband, who ran her business in her absence,

Workers packing boxes for Elizabeth Arden cosmetics in 1944 *(Library of Congress)*

finally arranged to have his wife moved to a prison in France. At the end of the war, she resumed her important role in the Elizabeth Arden Company. Although Arden could not secure her sister's release, she did bring other European employees and their relatives to safety in the United States.

After the war, Arden continued to expand her product line. She had earlier added lingerie and accessories to her salons

Arden with one of her racing horses in 1959. *(Courtesy of Alfred Eisenstaedt/Time & Life Pictures/Getty Images)*

and in 1945 introduced fashion clothing and marketed them to fine department stores. Through the years, she helped launch the careers of several designers, including Oscar de la Renta.

One of Arden's greatest personal losses came after the war. In 1946, twenty-two of her thoroughbreds perished in a fire at Arlington Park in Chicago. During the 1940s, however, her racing horses began to turn a profit. She hired "Silent" Tom Smith, who had trained the great horse Seabiscuit. In May 1947, her horse Jet Pilot won the Kentucky Derby at Churchill Downs in Louisville, Kentucky. Her success in horse racing finally brought her acceptance into the exclusive society of the Vanderbilts and Whitneys, who also owned horses.

The 1950s saw the rise of a youth market in the cosmetics industry. Charles Revson, head of Revlon, went after this middle-class market. His "Fire and Ice" line of lipstick and polish was extremely successful and he expanded his company. Arden and Rubinstein stuck with their upper-scale customers, but newcomer Estée Lauder began to threaten their hegemony. The two elderly beauty queens did not easily surrender their niche in the market place.

As Arden entered the 1960s, now in her eighties, she continued to travel and socialize at a frenetic pace. She opened a new luxury salon in Chicago, and bought a castle in Ireland where she quartered some of her horses. Syracuse University honored her with a Doctor of Law degree; she now had her coveted college diploma. But she also experienced some tragedies. Her horses lost money, trusted aides retired, and friends died. She mourned the passing scene. "I don't think society means a thing anymore," she said. "I've even noticed it with the horses."

Arden on the cover of *Time Magazine* in 1946. *(Courtesy of Time Life Pictures/ Getty Images)*

The face of the future

...luminous, lovely—with Elizabeth Arden's new Illusion Foundation

A new look in faces—smooth, mysterious, lustrous—to make yesterday's make-up seem dated. Soft though it feels, finely though it floats over your skin, Illusion gives magical cover and colour with a beautiful opalescent lustre. The look of the future is here to-day with Illusion, in nine natural shades, all at their loveliest with Elizabeth Arden's new Transparent Powder.

Elizabeth Arden

A 1968 magazine advertisement for Elizabeth Arden products *(Courtesy of Antiques & Collectables/Alamy)*

Arden started the decade physically fit, but soon began to experience health problems. By 1964, she had suffered a series of minor strokes. Two years later, she had a serious fall in Dublin, Ireland. She died October 18, 1966, in New York City, at the age of eighty-four. At the time of her death, Elizabeth Arden remained the sole shareholder of her company. She died one of the richest women in the world.

In her will, Arden left $4 million to her sister Gladys. To her niece, Patricia Young, she gave $2 million, plus all her jewelry, personal effects, and most of her estate. She left $4 million to her employees. Unfortunately, beneficiaries had to wait years to collect because the United States government presented a tax bill for more than $35 million. She had refused to set up trusts or tax-sheltered foundations. To pay this enormous debt, the company sold off Arden's horses and properties and it took five years to settle her estate.

Today, her former blue-grass estate is used by the University of Kentucky for equine research—a project she would have approved. After passing through the hands of several firms, Elizabeth Arden, Inc. is now owned by FFI Fragrances. Her Eight Hour Cream remains a best seller to this day. The fact that her empire still endures would have pleased her most of all. She once said to an interviewer, "Isn't it remarkable what a woman can do with a little ambition."

Elizabeth Arden timeline

1881   Born Florence Nightingale Graham in Woodbridge, Ontario, on December 31.

1907   Moves to New York City.

1910   Chooses the Elizabeth Arden trade name.

1910   Opens first beauty salon on Fifth Avenue in New York.

1914   Expands salon business to Washington, D.C.

1915   Marries Thomas Jenkins Lewis.

1922   Introduces salon in London, England.

1924   Opens salon in Paris, France.

1929   Launches four fragrances.

1934   Opens luxury spa Maine Chance in Mount Vernon, Maine; divorces Thomas Lewis.

1942   Marries Prince Michael Evlanoff.

1945   Introduces brand of designer clothes.

1947   Her horse Jet Pilot wins the Kentucky Derby.

1966   Dies in New York City, on October 18.

SEVEN

Estée Lauder

*E*stée Lauder demanded high standards of quality and excellence. "Good was not good enough," she said in her autobiography. "I could always make it better."

Born Josephine Esther Mentzer ("Estée") to Jewish immigrants Rose and Max Mentzer in Corona, Queens, New York, she listed her birth date as July 1, 1908, although her family said it was two years earlier. When her father enrolled her in school, he called her "Esty," but school officials wrote down Estée and it stuck.

Most of her life, Estée led people to believe that her birth place was Vienna, Austria, and that she was reared in Flushing, Long Island, the child of wealthy parents. In reality, she grew up above her father's hardware store in Queens, a working-class Italian neighborhood at the time. Estée worked in her father's store where she arranged wares and created window displays. She enjoyed wrapping the Christmas gifts of hammer and nails that her father gave to customers. She later claimed that her perfectionist tendencies came from her father. "I . . . inherited his genes for high standards—things must be perfect to be acceptable," she said.

Estée learned about beauty products and fine clothes from her mother. Rose Schotz Mentzer, ten years older than her husband, wore fine clothes and took great care of her skin. Estée liked to watch her mother's beauty ritual. Even as a young child, she enjoyed brushing her mother's and sister's hair and loved applying their facial creams.

Estée had a large extended family, which included older sister Renee, and five half-brothers and one half-sister from her mother's first marriage. Across the street from the hardware store was the department store Plafker and Rosenthal, owned by Estée's half-brother and his partner. The half-brother's wife Fanny and her sister Frieda ran the store. They indulged Estée by letting her try on beautiful clothes. They also let her wait on customers. Lauder later said she learned about business from these two women.

John Schotz, her maternal uncle, a Hungarian immigrant and chemist, had a business that interested her more than retail, however. In 1924, he established New Way Laboratory, where he made cold creams under the label Floranna, his wife's name, as well as toothpaste, dog mange medicine, paint remover, and mustache wax. Estée was fascinated by Uncle John's concoctions, and he taught her how to mix ingredients for his facial creams.

At about the age of sixteen, Estée, her mother, and her sister went to stay with her aunt in Milwaukee to escape a polio epidemic sweeping New York. There, after school, she worked in a beauty parlor, cleaning combs and brushes. She also sold Uncle John's cold creams in the beauty shop and gave facial massages. After she returned home to New York, she continued selling her uncle's facial products.

Estée Mentzer grew into a lovely young woman with blond hair, hazel eyes, high cheekbones, and flawless skin. Her good looks and outgoing personality attracted the attentions of twenty-five-year-old Joseph Lauter, later changed to Lauder. The couple married in January 1930. She put on lipstick before her wedding, but her father made her rub most of it off; he believed that proper women should not wear paint. She gave birth to her first son Leonard three years later.

To maintain her blond hair, Lauder had it done regularly at the beauty shop of Florence Morris. One day, the owner asked her, "What do you do to keep your skin looking so fresh and lovely?" At her next appointment, Lauder brought four jars of creams and lotions, all made from her uncle's formula, and smeared then on Morris's skin. After removing the creams, she also applied three of her own products: blush, powder, and lipstick. Impressed, the owner asked if Lauder would open a concession at her new salon on East Sixtieth Street. Lauder agreed, and started selling her creams behind the counter.

Lauder did not wait for the salon patrons to come to her; she took her products directly to the customers. She knew that when a woman sat under the hair dryer she was often bored. She approached the ladies and asked permission to apply some of her special cream to the woman's face. When the customer's hair dried, Lauder would remove the cream and quickly apply her own makeup, all within three minutes. The woman usually purchased the products, but even if she did not buy, Lauder would give her a small, free sample. She knew that if she could convince a woman to try a product, she would later become a lifelong customer.

Another beauty salon asked Lauder to sell her products, and she soon expanded to even more shops. She hired saleswomen and trained them how to get the best results. She was picky about whom she hired, wanting young, attractive women who had outgoing, but non-aggressive personalities. She hired about one in twenty women who applied. Lauder made regular checkups to see that the saleswomen demonstrated the products correctly.

Lauder was an aggressive and relentless seller herself. During the summer, she sold her products at resort hotels on Long Island, New York. Later, she sold her goods in Miami, Florida. Everywhere she went, she carried free samples in her purse. She even stopped women on the street and on trains and gave them beauty tips, suggesting they try her products and pressing free samples into their hands. While in Florida, she once approached a Salvation Army sister and told her that she could serve the Lord and still be attractive. Then, Lauder showed her how.

Lauder loved people and parties, while her husband Joe was quiet and reserved, and preferred to spend his evenings at home. Estée Lauder had a busy travel schedule, promoting her products; eventually the Lauder's marriage began to suffer. She asked for a divorce in 1939 but after three years she realized she had made a big mistake. "I don't know why I broke up with him," she told a friend. The couple remarried in 1942, and two years later, their second son Ronald was born.

In 1946, the Lauders decided to put all their assets in Estée's products. Her father also invested. The *New York Times* stated that she received financial backing from her friend Arnold L. van Ameringen, a Dutch industrialist and head of International Flavors and Fragrances (IFF). Still, even with sufficient financial resources, the Lauders' lawyer and accountant tried to talk them out of starting the business venture. Lauder would be competing against long-established firms such as Elizabeth Arden, Helena Rubinstein, and Revlon. However, Estée never doubted that she would be successful. "Risk taking is the cornerstone of empires," she said. "No one ever became a success without taking chances." She visualized success—and then worked hard for it.

The company began with Estée Lauder as chief executive officer and with her name on the products. Joe Lauder handled finances and production, while she took care of marketing and sales. They rented a former restaurant to manufacture products. She started with four items: two creams, a cleansing oil, and a lotion. All were based from her uncle's original formula, with improvements she had made. "We were selling jars of hope," she said.

Lauder originally put her creams in white jars with black lids, but changed her packaging because of an accident. A friend had purchased several jars of Lauder's creams and stored them in her refrigerator. The cold and dampness caused the Estée Lauder labels to come off. A maid, preparing for a dinner party, saw the white jars, and assumed they contained mayonnaise. She added seasonings and served it as salad dressing. None of the guests became ill, though the hostess nearly died from embarrassment. Lauder decided to put her creams in light blue-green jars with her name embossed *into* the glass. She chose this color because she thought it would go well with most bathroom wallpaper. This turquoise shade also suggested elegance, and it was her favorite color.

Lauder insisted every product made be of the highest quality. If quality came first, then sales would follow. She also paid much attention to her packaging, containers, boxes, wrapping paper, all of which cost more than the ingredients. She said, "I learned early that being a perfectionist and providing quality was the only way to do business."

From the beginning, Lauder targeted an upscale clientèle and wanted to market her products in elite department stores. She hounded department store buyers to carry her line. Victory came in 1948 when she landed an account with Saks Fifth Avenue in New York City. Lauder also got her products placed at exclusive stores in other cities, including Neiman Marcus in Dallas, Texas. Stanley Marcus, then head of Neiman Marcus, called her a "determined" saleswoman. Lauder attributed her success to her persistence.

After she landed an account, she fought for the most desirable spot at the cosmetics counter. She had noticed that when women entered a department store they first looked to the right. Lauder demanded—and got—the right front counter space for her brand. She also placed her products in other sections of the store, suntan creams in the swimsuit section and soaps with towel displays.

Lauder personally opened all the new markets herself. The week prior to opening, she traveled to the new store, hired, and trained saleswomen. For promotion, she met with editors of magazines and gave them three-minute facials and free samples. She also advertised her products in local newspapers and radios. On opening day, she stood at the counter and sold her wares. She loved to apply her products on customers' faces and making sales. "Selling, especially, is an art form that depends on spirit—and honesty," she said. Each day, Lauder always set a sales goal for herself. She liked to tell the story about a new store opening in Houston. At the

Lauder was able to get her products placed in upscale stores like Neiman Marcus. Stanley Marcus, president of Neiman Marcus, referred to Lauder as a "determined" saleswoman. *(Courtesy of Nina Leen/ Time Life Pictures/Getty Images)*

end of the first day, she had done well but had not quite met her quota. She slipped off her shoes and prepared for the store to close. A woman happened to walk past the counter. In a flash, Lauder stepped back into her shoes and approached the potential customer. She made the sale and her $1,000 sales quota for the day.

During the early years, she spent a great deal of time on the road, building her business. One year, she spent twenty-five weeks traveling. "Business is a magnificent obsession," she wrote. "I've never been bored a day in my life." Back in New York, Joe Lauder kept the business running, working eleven hours a day, seven days a week. Their son Leonard delivered goods to Saks on his bicycle when not in school.

The Lauders started with $50,000 to put into advertising but could not find an ad agency that would take the small account. She decided to instead put this money into offering free samples of her best merchandise. One competitor predicted that she would fail because she gave away too much of her business. Charles of the Ritz cosmetics company had been the first cosmetic company to offer free samples, but Estée Lauder perfected this marketing tool. The free sample became permanently linked to her name and her business; it also became a common practice in the industry.

Like other competitors, Lauder decided to add fragrances to her products line. To develop a scent, she went to International Flavors and Fragrances (IFF). Ernest Shiftan, a chemist and perfumer with IFF, had one of the best "noses" in the business. An expert perfumer can detect 3,000 to 4,000 scents and can blend three hundred to four hundred natural and synthetic aromatics; it is a rare ability. Lauder, who had a perfumer's nose herself, worked with Shiftan on her new fragrance until she found what she wanted. She picked a warm, sweet smell and called it Youth Dew.

In 1953, Lauder launched Youth Dew, and it was an immediate success. She next brought the fragrance out as a bath oil. The oil mixed well with water and had a long-lasting effect because of a time-released formula. Youth Dew expanded to include perfume, cologne, lotion, powder, and deodorant.

Lauder wanted to convince women to buy and use fragrances as readily as they purchased and used lipsticks. She marketed Youth Dew wherever she went. When she first introduced the fragrance at New York's Bonwit Teller department store, she gave a tiny amount as a free sample. Of course, she wore the product herself. She also sprayed it on friends and in elevators. In Paris she "accidentally" spilled a bottle in a department store. "If you don't smell it, you can't sell it" was one of her favorite expressions. In customers' monthly bills, she included a small sample of fragrance sealed in a small glassine envelope. This was another new and clever marketing tool. By 1955, 80 percent of her business at Saks came from Youth Dew.

Like the other beauty queens, Estée courted the media. She carefully cultivated her company's image and her own—they were one and the same. She charmed the press, telling amusing stories. However, she never talked much about herself. When she did, she told reporters only what she wanted them to know. Interviewers had trouble getting personal details. One journalist wrote that obtaining information from Estée Lauder was "akin to penetrating a stone wall with a needle."

By the mid-1960s, Lauder's rivals Helena Rubinstein and Elizabeth Arden had died. Charles Revson, who headed Revlon, remained. Lauder and Revson loathed one another. He vowed to "bury her." His company had sales and advertising budgets seven to eight times larger than Lauder's. She knew better than to go head-to-head against Revlon. Instead, she would bring out a product and wait for it to catch on in the market place. Revson would watch for her latest offering and then launch a similar product. She accused him of planting spies in her company.

Estée Lauder *(Courtesy of Evening Standard/Getty Images)*

The company developed a new, elaborate coding system to foil any spies. According to Lauder, when she wanted a new fragrance, she had IFF develop 95 to 98 percent of the perfume, later she added the rest. Only Estée, Joe, and Leonard knew the remaining secret ingredients. Even after she retired as chief executive officer, the company consulted her when they wanted to add a new scent to a product.

From the beginning, the Lauders had groomed their son Leonard to help with the business. In college, his parents sent him all the company's business memos and correspondence. After graduation, he joined the United States Navy as a supply officer, and he formally joined the company in 1958. Soon he was an expert in marketing and advertising. At his suggestion, Estée Lauder expanded internationally, first into Canada in 1958 and two years later to England. He also had the idea for Clinique, the company's most successful product.

Clinique, developed in great secrecy, came on the market in 1968 as a non-allergenic skin-care product. Daughter-in-law Evelyn Lauder suggested the name Clinique because it was a scientific sounding name. They formed a separate company to make and market Clinique. Ronald Lauder assumed duties as executive vice-president, and later president, of the new company. Like most of its products, the Estée Lauder firm waited for its latest line to catch on in the market place. It took four years before Clinique showed a profit.

Estée Lauder had placed her immediate family in top management of the company. However, family members did not get their positions because of their name. They had to work their way up and prove their business skills. She believed in hiring people who shared her philosophy and who took risks. She sought aggressive, creative people. Although she admitted that she was a demanding taskmaster, she respected her employees and paid them well. "Hire people who think as you do and treat them well. In our business, they are top priority."

With her sons now managing the business, Lauder had more time to enjoy the finest things money could buy. She spent time at her homes in the south of France and in Palm

Lauder with her husband Joseph (left) and their son Ronald *(Courtesy of Morgan Collection/Getty Images)*

Beach, Florida. Her house in New York City looked like a Venetian palace. She loved to have parties and planned black-tie dinners with her usual perfectionist attention to detail. Her tables had elaborate settings, and she picked formal gowns to match her party theme and decor. "I invest more time and diligence to present the perfect event, than most people invest in planning their daughter's wedding," she said. "If you do anything, do it right."

Lauder loved to mingle with the rich and the famous. She aggressively cultivated friendships with certain people, such as the Duke and Duchess of Windsor and Princess Grace of Monaco. "For all her pushing, you couldn't but help admire Estée Lauder," a friend commented.

Lauder cultivated friendships with wealthy, famous people like Princess Grace of Monaco. *(Courtesy of AP Images)*

Lauder and Joseph tour a newly opened playground in New York's Central Park whose construction was sponsored by the Estée and Joseph Lauder Foundation. *(Courtesy of AP Images)*

Estée Lauder supported various charities. She gave to the Red Cross and contributed to the restoration of the Palace of Versailles in France. She also donated to the Museum of American Art and the Whitney Museum of Modern Art. The Estée and Joseph Lauder Foundation, created in 1962, sponsored three children's playgrounds in New York's Central Park. Today, her foundation actively supports breast cancer research.

In January 1982, Joe Lauder died of a heart attack. His death devastated his wife. She dedicated her 1985 autobiography to her husband, calling him, "my balance." He had always supported her and had taken great pride in her accomplishments. Estée Lauder said she could not have built her empire without him. To honor his memory, she and her family created the Joseph H. Lauder Institute of Management and International Studies at the University of Pennsylvania.

In 1993, the firm conferred Estée Lauder with the title of founding chairwoman. Two years later, she officially retired. In 1995, the company began selling shares of stock on the

Lauder (center) at the opening of an Estée Lauder store in 1989 *(Courtesy of AFP/Getty Images)*

New York Stock Exchange, though the family retained a vast majority of the shares. Lauder never lost her love of selling. Into her eighties, she would walk into her grandson's store and demonstrate how he should sell his products.

Estée Lauder died April 24, 2004, in Manhattan. Her obituary in the *New York Times* gave her age as ninety-seven. At the time of her death, Estée Lauder, International had about 2,000 products, which were sold in more than 130 countries. Its founder had won many awards, including the French Legion of Honor and the United States Presidential Medal of Freedom. The firm is now passing into the hands of the third generation of the Lauder family.

About her business success, Lauder said, "Anyone who wants to achieve a dream must stay strong, focused and steady. She must expect and demand perfection and never settle for mediocrity."

Estée Lauder timeline

1908 Born Josephine Esther Mentzer in Corona, Queens, New York, on July 1.

1930 Marries Joseph Lauter (Lauder).

1933 Son Leonard is born.

1939 Divorces Joseph Lauder.

1942 Remarries Joseph Lauder.

1944 Son Ronald is born.

1946 Forms Estée Lauder Company.

1948 Lands account at Saks Fifth Avenue, New York.

1953 Launches Youth Dew fragrance.

1958 Expands market into Canada.

1968 Introduces Clinique.

1973 Steps aside to become chair of company; Leonard Lauder becomes president of Estée Lauder, International.

1982 Joseph Lauder dies.

1993   Named founding chairwoman of her firm.

2004   Dies in Manhattan, New York, on April 24.

Sources

CHAPTER ONE: Beauty and Business

p. 17, "What every woman . . . " A'Lelia Bundles, *On Her Own Ground: The Life and Times of Madam C. J. Walker* (New York: Scribner, 2001), 77.

CHAPTER TWO: Martha Matilda Harper

p. 24, "Beauty and health . . . " Jane Plitt, *Martha Matilda Harper:How One Woman Changed the Face of Business* (Syracuse, NY: Syracuse University Press, 2000), 48.

p. 26, "Not just a hairdo . . . " Karen Thure, "Martha Harper pioneered in the hair business," *Smithsonian* (September 1976), 100.

p. 30, "Build everything on service . . . " Lucile Huntington, "Founder of Harper Method Shops Helps Many Gain Business Independence," *Christian Science Monitor,* March 5, 1946, 11.

p. 30, "take people the way . . ." Ibid., 11

p. 31, "Robbie always looks out . . . " Thure, "Martha Harper pioneered in the hair business," 99.

p. 32, "We have laid a foundation . . . " Plitt, *Martha Matilda Harper,* 109.

p. 34, "The Harper Method . . . " Ibid., 126.

p. 36, "The child in your shop . . . " Ibid., 116.

p. 36, "HARPER SERVICE COSTS . . . " Ibid., 128.

p. 38, "The Great Achievement . . ." Plitt, *Martha Matilda Harper*, 114.

CHAPTER THREE: Annie Turnbo Malone

p. 41, "my folks wanted. . ." Gwendolyn Robinson, "Class, Race, and Gender: A Transcultural Theoretical and Sociohistorical Analysis of Cosmetic Institutions and Practices to 1920" (master's thesis, University of Illinois at Chicago, 1984), 348.

p. 42, "When I was a little . . ." Ibid.

p. 44, "I went out . . ." J. L. Wilkerson, *Story of Pride, Power and Uplift: Annie T. Malone* (Kansas City, MO: Acorn Books, 2003), 22.

p. 44, "to interfere . . ." Robinson, "Class, Race, and Gender," 349.

p. 47, "The proof of the value . . . " "Poro ad," *St. Louis Palladium,* April 27, 1907.

p. 48, "progressive businesswoman . . . " Bundles, *On her Own Ground*, 149.

p. 51, "To lend charm and beauty . . . " "Poro's Purpose," Chicago Historical Society, Barnett Collection, Box 262, folder 5, 1925.

p. 52, "I urge you . . . " "Poro College brochure," Chicago Historical Society, Barnett Collection, Box 262, folder 7.

p. 52, "It is our earnest wish . . . " "Poro College brochure."

p. 53, "belonged to God . . ." Robinson, "Class, Race, and Gender," 357.

p. 55, "The entry of . . . " "Poro's Purpose."

p. 55, "That college . . ." "Says Husband was Poro Figurehead," *St. Louis Globe Democrat*, January 15, 1927.

p. 56, "That you are a splendid . . ." Claude A. Barnett, "Letter to Annie Malone," February 29, 1929.

p. 56, "Make the ad so . . . " Susannah Walker, *Style & Status: Selling Beauty to African American Women,*

1920-1975 (Lexington: University Press of Kentucky, 2007), 11.

p. 56, "competition from white . . ." Ibid., 10.

p. 58, "It is regrettable . . ." C. C. Spaulding, "Letter to Claude A. Barnett," October 6, 1939.

p. 59, "I have not been seeking . . ." Robinson, "Class, Race, and Gender," 356.

p. 59, "Annie Malone's life . . . " Harold Keith, "Annie M. Turnbo Malone," *Pittsburgh Courier,* August 10, 1957, 4.

CHAPTER FOUR: Madam C. J. Walker

p. 63, "Surely, you . . . " A'Lelia Bundles, *Madam C. J. Walker* (Philadelphia: Chelsea House Publishers, 1991), 13.

p. 68, "What are you . . . " A'Lelia Bundles, *On Her Own Ground*, 48.

p. 68, "A big, black . . ." Robinson, "Class, Race, and Gender," 379.

p. 70, "All the people . . ." Bundles, *On Her Own Ground*, 93.

p. 71, "I want . . . " Della Yannuzzi, *Madam C. J. Walker: Self-Made Businesswoman* (Berkeley Heights, NJ: Enslow Publishers, Inc., 2000), 31, 33.

p. 76, "one of the most . . . " Bundles, *Madam C. J. Walker*, 17.

p. 78, "you have opened . . ." Robinson, "Class, Race, and Gender," 385.

p. 78-79, "We should protest . . . " Bundles, *On her Own Ground*, 212.

p. 79, "Thou Shall Not . . . " Yannuzzi, *Madam C. J. Walker: Self-Made Businesswoman*, 65.

p. 80, "My object . . . " A'Lelia Bundles, "Madam C. J. Walker," *American History* (August 1996), 47.

p. 80, "I want to live . . . " Bundles, *Madam C.J. Walker,* 102

p. 83, "I promoted myself . . ." Bundles, *Madam C. J. Walker*, 105.

CHAPTER FIVE: Helena Rubinstein

p. 86, "my own skin . . ." Lindy Woodhead, *War Paint: Madame Helena Rubinstein and Elizabeth Arden* (Hoboken, N.J.: John Wiley & Sons, Inc., 2003), 40.

p. 87, "I had to get to . . . " Patrick O'Higgins, *Madame: An Intimate Biography of Helena Rubinstein* (New York: The Viking Press, 1971), 147.

p. 93, "Here is not only . . ." Helena Rubinstein, *My Life For Beauty* (New York: Simon and Schuster, 1966), 58.

p. 95, "Madame liked the feeling . . ." O'Higgins, *Madame: An Intimate Biography of Helena Rubinstein*, 55.

p. 96, "I owe it . . . " Ibid., 143.

p. 97, "sunburn is beauty suicide . . . " Lindy Woodhead, *War Paint: Madame Helena Rubinstein and Miss Elizabeth Arden* (New York: John Wiley & Sons, Inc., 2003), 5.

p. 97, "Take advantage . . ." O'Higgins, *Madame: An Intimate Biography of Helena Rubinstein*, 153.

p. 97-98, "It keeps the wrinkles . . ." Helena Rubinstein, *My Life For Beauty*, 13.

p. 100, "A gift for you . . . " O'Higgins, *Madame: An Intimate Biography of Helena Rubinstein*, 119.

p. 100, "Good publicity . . ." Ibid., 145.

p. 102, "I'm an old woman . . ." *New York Times*, April 2, 1965.

p. 103, "I want the business . . ." O'Higgins, *Madame: An Intimate Biography of Helena Rubinstein*, 294.

CHAPTER SIX: Elizabeth Arden

p. 106, "I want to be . . . " Alfred Lewis and Constance Woodworth, *Miss Elizabeth Arden: An Untouched Portrait* (New York: Coward, McCann & Geoghegan, Inc., 1972), 34.

p. 110, "the way she could . . ." Ibid., 57.

p. 113, "that dreadful woman . . . " Ibid., 171.

p. 115, "Every woman has the right . . ." Ibid., 156.

p. 115, "I don't want . . . " Ibid., 206.

p. 116, "It's easy . . . " Ibid., 271.

p. 118, "My business is . . . " Woodhead, *War Paint: Madame Helena Rubinstein and Elizabeth Arden*, 297.

p. 118, "you've got to fight . . ." Lewis and Woodworth, *Miss Elizabeth Arden: An Untouched Portrait*, 237.

p. 122, "I don't think . . . " Woodhead, *War Paint: Madame Helena Rubinstein and Elizabeth Arden*, 386-387.

p. 125, "Isn't it remarkable . . . " Lewis and Woodworth, *Miss Elizabeth Arden: An Untouched Portrait*, 205.

CHAPTER SEVEN: Estée Lauder

p. 127, "Good was not good enough . . ." Estée Lauder, *Estée: A Success Story* (New York: Random House, 1985), 24.

p. 128, "I . . . inherited . . ." Ibid., 10.

p. 129, "What do you . . ." Ibid., 26.

p. 130, "I don't know why . . ." Richard Severo, "Estée Lauder, Pursuer of Beauty and Cosmetics Titan, Dies at 97," *New York Times*, April 26, 2004.

p. 131, "Risk taking . . . " Estée Lauder, *Estée: A Success Story*, 27.

p. 131, "We were selling . . . " Ibid., 51.

p. 132, "I learned early . . . " Ibid., 14.

p. 132, "Selling, especially . . . " Ibid., 67.

p. 134, "Business is . . . " Peter Krauss, *The Book of*

Business Wisdom (John Wiley & Sons, Inc., 1997), 349.

p. 135, "If you don't smell . . . " Lee Israel, *Estée Lauder: Beyond the Magic* (New York: Macmillan Publishing, 1985), 146.

p. 137, "Hire people . . . " Kraus, *The Book of Business Wisdom,* 353.

p. 139, "I invest more time . . ." Lauder, *Estée: A Success Story,* 187.

p. 139, "For all her . . ." Woodhead, *War Paint: Madame Helena Rubinstein and Elizabeth Arden,* 389.

p. 142, "Anyone who wants . . . " Lauder, *Estée: A Success Story,* 222.

Bibliography

Angeloglou, Maggie. *A History of Make-Up*. New York: Macmillan Press, 1970.

Banner, Lois. *American Beauty*. Chicago: University of Chicago Press, 1983.

Bender, Marilyn. *At the Top*. Garden City, New York: Doubleday & Company, Inc., 1985.

Berry, Chuck. *Chuck Berry*. New York: Harmony Books, 1987.

Brands, H. W. *Masters of Enterprise*. New York: The Free Press, 1999.

Bryer, Robin. *The History of Hair: Fashion and Fantasy Down the Ages*. London: Philip Wilson Publishers, 2003.

Bundles, A'Lelia. "Madam C. J. Walker." *American History*, August 1996.

_____. *Madam C. J. Walker*. New York: Chelsea House Publishers, 1991.

_____. *On Her Own Ground: The Life and Times of Madam C. J. Walker*. New York: Scribner, 2001.

Claude A. Barnett Collection. Chicago Historical Society. Annie Turnbo-Malone File, Box 262.

Eddy, Mary Baker. *Rudimental Divine Science*. Boston: Trustees under the Will Of Mary Baker G. Eddy, 1906.

Gross, Daniel. *Forbes Greatest Business Stories of All Time*. New York: John Wiley & Sons, 1996.

Hine, Darlene, and Kathleen Thompson. *Black Women in America*. Bloomington: Indiana University Press, 1994.

Huntington, Lucile. "Founder of Harper Method Shops Helps Many Gain Business Independence." *Christian Science Monitor*, March 5, 1946.

Israel, Lee. *Estée Lauder: Beyond the Magic*. New York: Macmillan Publishing, 1985.

James, Edward T, ed. *Notable American Women, 1605-1959: A Biographical Dictionary*. Cambridge, Mass.: Belknap Press of Harvard University Press, 1971.

Keith, Harold. "Annie M. Turnbo Malone." *Pittsburgh Courier,* August 10, 1957.

Klein, Maury. *The Change Makers: From Carnegie to Gates, How the Great Entrepreneurs Transformed Ideas into Industries*. New York: Henry Holt and Company, 2003.

Krauss, Peter, ed. *The Book of Business Wisdom*. New York: John Wiley & Sons, Inc., 1997.

Lauder, Estée. *Estée: A Success Story*. New York: Random House, 1985.

Lewis, Alfred, and Constance Woodworth. *Miss Elizabeth Arden*. New York: Coward, McCann & Geoghegan, Inc., 1972.

Lockwood, Leonard. "Beauty Was Her Business." *Democrat and Chronicle*, February 23, 1963.

Markey, Kevin. *100 Most Important Women in the 20th Century*. Des Moines, Iowa: Ladies Home Journal Books, 1998.

Obituary of Helena Rubinstein. *New York Times,* April 2, 1965.

Obituary of Martha M. Harper. *New York Times*, August 5, 1950.

Morgan, Thelma, ed. *Profiles in Silhouette: The Contributions of Black Women of Missouri*. St. Louis: The St. Louis Alumnae Chapter of Delta Sigma Theta, Inc., 1980.

Morrow, Willie. *400 Years Without a Comb*. San Diego: Black Publishers of San Diego, 1973.

The National Cyclopaedia of American Biography. Vol. 39. New York: James T. White & Company, 1954.

O' Higgins, Patrick. *Madame: An Intimate Biography of Helena Rubinstein.* London: Weidenfeld and Nicholson, 1971.

Peiss, Kathy. *Hope in a Jar.* New York: Henry Holt and Company, 1998.

Plitt, Jane. *Martha Harper and the American Dream: How One Woman Changed the Face of Modern Business.* Syracuse, New York: Syracuse University Press, 2000.

Robinson Gwendolyn. *Class, Race and Gender: A Transcultural Theoretical and Sociohistorical Analysis of Cosmetics Institutions and Practices to 1920.* Thesis., University of Illinois at Chicago, 1984.

Robinson, Julian. *The Quest for Human Beauty*, New York: W. W. Norton & Company, 1998.

Rubinstein, Helena. *My Life for Beauty.* London: The Bodley Head, 1964.

_____. *The Art of Feminine Beauty.* New York: Horace Liveright, 1930.

Sicherman, Barbara, et al. *Notable American Women: The Modern Period.* Cambridge, Mass.: Belknap Press of Harvard University Press, 1980.

Sluby, Patricia. *The Inventive Spirit of African Americans: Patented Ingenuity.* Westport, Conn.: Praeger, 2004.

Stanley, Marcus. *Minding the Store.* Boston: Little, Brown and Company, 1974.

Thure, Karen. "Martha Harper pioneered the hair business." *Smithsonian Magazine*, September 1976.

Tobias, Andrew. *Fire and Ice: The Story of Charles Revson—the Man Who Built The Revlon Empire.* New York: William Morrow and Company, Inc., 1976.

Walker, Susannah. *Style & Status: Selling Beauty to*

African American Women, 1920-1975. Lexington: University Press of Kentucky, 2007.

Wilkerson, J. L. *Story of Pride, Power and Uplift: Annie T. Malone.* Kansas City, Missouri: Acorn Press, 2003.

Woodhead, Lindy. *War Paint: Madame Helena Rubinstein and Miss Elizabeth Arden.* New York: John Wiley & Sons, Inc., 2003.

Yannuzzi, Della. *Madam C. J. Walker: Self-Made Businesswoman.* Berkeley Heights, N. J.: Enslow Publishers, Inc., 2000.

Web sites

http://www.marthamatildaharper.com
Site contains brief biography of Martha Matilda Harper, as well as research information and book reviews.

http://www.csupomona.edu/~plin/inventors/malone.html
Annie Malone biography, references, and links to other Web sites about her.

http://www.madamcjwalker.com
Madam C. J. Walker Web site maintained by her great-grand-daughter. Includes suggested reading list, answers to frequently asked questions, and brief biography.

http://www.elizabetharden.com
Web site gives Elizabeth Arden heritage, beauty products, Red Door spas.

http://www.esteelauder.com
Information about history of Estée Lauder, product lines, and the company.

http://www.helenarubinsteinfdn.org/about.html
Maintained by the Helena Rubinstein Foundation, this Web site features a profile of the organization's founder, as well as information about the various programs that the foundation supports.

http://www.jewishvirtuallibrary.org/jsource/biography/bio-women.html
Here, on the Jewish Virtual Library, you will find brief biographies of both Helena Rubinstein and Estee Lauder. The library is a division of the American-Israeli Cooperative Enterprise.

Index